Practicing From The Heart

In the age of technology

Practicing From The Heart

In the age of technology

Reza Ghadimi

Salutation

To all healthcare providers of all backgrounds
who provide for our fellow man around the globe.
From small villages and huts in remote corners of the
world to major medical centers and universities.
To frontline responders caring for sufferers of pandemics,
casualties of wars, victims of violent crimes and many
emergencies at the risk of their own well-being.

To my wife Kate, whose understanding and
support made my experiences possible.

Acknowledgment

My father; Zabihollah Ghadimi was a journalist, historian and writer. Much of my childhood was spent in print shops, so much so that my classmates often teased me of smelling of ink. I learned to operate a print press long before driving a car and to proofread before algebra and long division.

Early in my life I developed a habit of making notes on my encounters with people and places. A habit that came useful in my medical work. I have written much throughout my life about many experiences, studies and observations. Although I feel incompetent in dealing with the workings of today's computer technologies, I purchased one of the first home computers on the market – a Radio Shack TRS 80. Using it was a godsend that has helped me with my writings to this date.

Foreword to "Practicing from the Heart"
By Dr. Humayun (Hank) Chaudhry

Reza Ghadimi is at least two decades older than me but I have known him for more than a decade and we share much in common.

We both immigrated to the United States in our youth (Reza at age 17, me at age 5), we both completed our health professions education here (Reza became a physician assistant, I became a general internist), we both did part of our training in New York's South Bronx (Reza at Lincoln Hospital, me at St. Barnabas Hospital), we both served in the United States Air Force (Reza as a medic, me as a flight surgeon in the reserves), and we both enjoy writing.

As he vividly recalls in his insightful memoir, "Practicing from the Heart," Reza has seen much of the world over the last 75 years, giving him an opportunity to observe and reflect on matters as varied as astronomy, religion, philosophy, sociology, psychology, and poetry, to name just a few disciplines. His collection of short articles in this laudable book covers these topics and more but his primary focus, as he also writes on his blog (The HealthCare PULSE, at www.thpulse.com), is to always be an "advocate of the poor and the homeless everywhere."

Reza learns in his teenage years from a friend of the family who is a doctor that the practice of medicine first and foremost involves the "art of listening, sensing, looking, and finally examining." The words echo those of Sir William Osler, the father of modern medicine, who famously said, "The whole art of medicine is in observation… but to educate the eye to see, the ear to hear and the finger to feel takes time, and to make a beginning, to start a man on the right path, is all that you can do." That same point is reinforced for Reza by a brusque nurse he encounters who says, "The most important thing is to listen to the patient."

Particularly poignant in this book are the stories Reza shares of weaknesses and failures, and of challenges and inadequacies, in our health care system for those who lack health insurance, for those who are undocumented, or for those with cultural backgrounds that are not always understood or appreciated. The story of an asthmatic mother of three who dies because she is unable to get the care that she needs on a timely basis is a reminder of what we still lack in health care, despite incredible advances over the last five decades in diagnostics and therapeutics. Reza admits he doesn't have specific solutions to all of these dilemmas, though he suggests technology and better communication will be critical factors that will enable improvement. While acknowledging that "legal minds" and "bean counters" will also need to figure some of these problems out, Reza's compassion is fully on display as he repeatedly suggests a sense of urgency to do something sooner rather than later to improve humanity.

The people he writes about or quotes in his short stories tell us a lot about Reza's own humanity and character. He mentions being inspired by luminaries like Pulitzer Prize-winning poet Maya Angelou, with whom he has a memorable conversation. But he also admiringly mentions a young man he meets early in life named Ibrahim, a surgical assistant he meets overseas who appears to lack a formal education (despite his work in the hospital) but always prays for the patients he helps manage. "The human body is sacred," Ibrahim tells Reza. "The very breath of God has given it life, treat it with reverence and respect and it will repay you by living well."

Reza demonstrates an exceptional curiosity about mankind and its place in the cosmos. When Halley's Comet makes its pass in 1986, many of us in North America were unable to see it well on terra firma because of where we were, due to bad weather or just too many city lights. Reza, too, had difficulty seeing it from the ground but that did not stop him. He did something many of us did not or could not do, hopping onto a Cessna plane (Reza is a licensed pilot) to get a closer view for himself at nightfall. He also marvels and talks about the lunar eclipse of the sun he witnesses and what it means to him.

Now retired from clinical practice, Reza is thinking a great deal about what is happening on the ground and what is in store for the future of medicine, especially with the COVID-19 pandemic all around us. He recognizes that, especially in the United States, we still have far to go to address inequities in health care, to improve the lot of tens of millions of individuals who lack health insurance, and provide broadband internet access across many more parts of the country, especially in rural areas. This latter point is of special interest to Reza, who has lived and worked in New Mexico for many years and has been active with the American Telemedicine Association (ATA). Reza even manages to mention, in passing, the future role that advances as 3-D printing, robotics and artificial (or augmented) intelligence may play to advance telemedicine and telehealth.

Having served on the New Mexico Medical Board for many years, Reza smartly reflects on what medical regulators may be able to do to advance the practice of medicine in the years ahead. He applauds efforts by state medical boards to support medical licensure portability, such as with the Interstate Medical Licensure Compact that has been promoted by the Federation of State Medical Boards and has thus far been passed into law by 29 states and two U.S. territories (including the District of Columbia). He notes that all health care providers need to do a better job in communicating with their patients, accurately observing that many of the complaints that state medical boards receive about inadequate or poor care by physicians and physician assistants could have been avoided through better communication between provider and patient.

Midway through his collection of stories, Reza waxes philosophically to consider a famous question attributed to the poet Cicero. "What greater or better gift can we offer the Republic," the Roman statesman asked more than two millennia ago, "than to teach our youth?" Reza's book does a splendid job, his gift to us, of teaching what matters most (humanity, fairness, tolerance, compassion, education, understanding, and technology) as we consider our future.

Humayun J. Chaudhry, DO, MACP, FRCP
President and CEO
Federation of State Medical Boards

June 26, 2020
Washington, DC

Endorsement

July 27, 2020

In Practicing from the Heart, Reza Ghadimi has captured the true heart of our healing profession through vignettes that are poignant and deeply moving. Reflecting on his life's calling, from working in small villages in several countries to Manhattan, Reza has offered up a global view of the tragedy of health disparities to the heroics of compassionate and altruistic health professionals.

Reza speaks of love and politics, conflicts and the brother and sister-hood that is the cornerstone of Medicine. He paints a stark and compelling contrast of the beauty of mankind and its brutality through the eyes of a caring practitioner of the healing arts. Every student thinking of entering the health professions should read this book.

Sincerely,
Paul B. Roth, MD, MS, F ACEP
Chancellor, UNM Health Sciences Center
CEO, UNM Health System

NOTICE

Many of the stories and essays in this book are my observations of other's works or may be based on stories I have heard. In no way are they an endorsement of their techniques nor are they suggested as a treatment method. They are simply a study of many people from different cultures caring for their needy.

Furthermore, I have been deliberately vague in describing them as I cannot remember particulars of their process or ingredients of the potion. These people usually have years of training by their instructors, mentors and elders in the particular use of herbs, concoctions, techniques and manipulative works. None should be used by anyone in treatment of patients.

It has become appallingly obvious that our technology has exceeded our humanity.

Albert Einstein

Contents

Introduction

When I entered the world of medicine some sixty-three years ago, medicine was considered to be about the most sacred thing in the world. The purpose was to help people and to do some good in the world. Money was never an issue till all of that changed in the 1980s with the privatization of healthcare. Since then it has become all about making money and less and less about caring for people. Today many still enter the profession with the true desire to help others. But the high cost of medical school and education soon make them question their choice. The for-profit establishment however, keeps telling them of how much money they are going to make and that all will be worth it. So they struggle through and graduate with a large debt to the very institution that hires them to make money for them. Before long, they find themselves processing patients through the conveyor belt of tests, referrals from one clinic to the next and one specialist to another. They go home exhausted and not even remembering whom they saw and whether they did anyone any good or not. Many get so entangled in this financial web that they either quit all together, get dependent on alcohol or drugs, or worse commit suicide. Our profession, which use to be one of the most rewarding careers, now has the dreaded distinction of having one of the highest rates of suicide.

I recall an occasion when a colleague/friend working at an industrial clinic lost two of her partners. She asked if I could help her till new doctors could be hired. I spent a few days with her and then was sent for an interview with the clinic CEO/manager.

"I've heard a lot about you and looking forward to have you working with us." He started and with the very next breath asked: "How many patients do you think you can see in an hour?"

I was dumbfounded. Once I regained my composure, I stood up and said: "If that is the very first question you are going to ask me, I don't think I could see enough to satisfy you." And walked out.

In other times, working at an urgent care or clinic run by a managed care organization, I would repeatedly be told: "It doesn't take 25 minutes to treat a cold!" In response, I would snap back that "I wasn't treating a cold, I was treating a person with a cold." In this book I reveal what a rewarding calling medicine use to be and how one can still make it so, even in this age of technology. This book has been in the writing for a long time. All through my years of practice in many roles, I routinely made notes of the interesting cases, people, places and times. Something I encourage everyone of you to get in the habit of doing especially if you are new in your career. I promise that it will be very rewarding.

Before I go any further, I would like to clarify a few points. Many who have read my writings, occasionally ask for clarity in my stories, the places they happened, the people involved and the times . But I have left many of these questions unanswered deliberately. My experiences have shown that when too much detail is given to a particularity, it diverts the reader's focus on a digression and away from the message at hand. This book is not about me or any particular person, place or time. Rather it is a message. A message on how to be a healer, a healthcare provider, a source of solace and a sanctuary of hope – a curandero. You may not get rich but will be content, satisfied and happy.

Most articles, essays and vignettes are the collection of experiences gained by me, but not all the stories are mine. I may have used the knowledge and stories of colleagues or of those told to me. I have jumbled some together in order to get a point across. So don't attribute everything to me and me alone. They are seventy-seven years of life's experience, seen, heard and practiced around this world.

Looking back, I should expect to see a life in a straight path, instead I am glad to find a meandering river of opportunities and pandemonium. A straight path would have missed the many fascinating things I've seen around the bends and twists of the river of life. The many people I've cared for in all corners of this world, their customs and traditions. Those I helped, and the ones I couldn't. The countless who were cured and the ones lost. The ones who became my friends and those who hated my guts. But that's life, one can only hope and pray to help more than not. So come along with me and share some of my experiences. You may agree with some of my decisions and disapprove of others. But I promise that you will not get bored.

Preface

My grandmother was a curandera – a medicine woman or a healer. I like the word curandera, because it means more than a medicine woman or a healer or any other English word used for such people. A curandera is more because such a person has power. Not just knowledge of medicine but the power and wisdom of knowing how to apply that knowledge to look into the inner soul of the sick and see what caused their illness.

Western medicine teaches us to treat the symptoms but not the person, it identifies illness as the failure of a specific organ to perform its task and therefore tries to set it right by fixing *it*. But the very existence of the human individual comprises the inseparable soul and spirit as well as the physical being. The inseparability of man's daily actions and behavior, however mundane, from his quintessential life escapes the way modern medicine treats people. It fails to appreciate the reason for a holistic approach to treating the sick, so that after an ill person is physically cured they may still be mentally drained and not fully recovered.

New Mexico, where I have lived for the past fifty years, is Indian country and many of the people we treat are Native Americans. Not understanding their culture can result in misinterpretation of their needs and their miscomprehension of our intent. So it takes a slightly different approach for us to serve these wonderful people. I love our Native people, as their traditions and outlook on life resemble much of what I was taught in my upbringing – half a world away.

A long time PA colleague, who also worked in some of the clinics on the reservations, tells a story that spotlights the message of this book nicely:

On one particular visit, his patient was an adorable boy of four who was there for a checkup. For the exam, he needed the child to disrobe which he did but refused to take his shoes off. His mother talked to him in their native tongue but to no avail. She finally informed my colleague that there was a hole in one of his socks and he was embarrassed to show it. My colleague says; I laughed heartily and sheepishly took my own shoe off and showed him a hole in *my* sock. He beamed gloriously and we became good friends to the delight of his mother.

No matter what our profession, we all strive to be the best and achieve stardom in our work. I don't know what 'reaching the summit of a profession' may mean to different people. It may be having a corner office on the top floor of a hospital overlooking Fifth Avenue and earning a seven-figure income or having tenure at a major medical school. Others may find it satisfying being CEO of a healthcare organization, group or business. Many judge their success in the amount of money they have made. But in the end when all is said and done, the plaques and awards put away, the bulging bank accounts passed on to our inheritors, we – needing the care of those we looked down on and who have taken over our corner office – find that no matter how successful we were in life it is the smiles and giggles of a little boy with a hole in his sock, laughing happily that will make us remember the good days, not the beaming faces of our financial managers.

Practicing from the Heart

ONE

FIRST JOB

Way back in the middle of the last century (circa 1958), a doctor friend of my father came over for dinner one summer night. In the tradition of the old days, they sat around talking about family, kids, politics and weather – we had no TV back then. Heck we had no electricity. I was a peewee fourteen-year-old boy who knew everything and was going to become a brain surgeon. Don't ask me why, but I suppose that the brain being in the head and the head being on top of the body, well that was as good a place to start as any.

So when the good doctor asked my father – they never talked to you directly – what *he* (my father) was going to have *me* study, my father answered that I was interested in becoming a doctor. Then he turned to me and asked; "Is that a fact?"

I sat up straight and put on a silly grin. "Yes, sir!" was my confident answer.

It so happened that our doctor friend was one of a few physicians who was part owner of a private hospital in our town.

"Well if that is the case," he said, "we better get you started. Since you are on summer break, why don't you come over to the hospital tomorrow and we'll see if we can get you a summer job. What do you think about that?" I wasn't expecting that, but was elated with the offer and said so. They went back to talking and I suddenly felt that I was not connected to the earth anymore.

Before leaving, our doctor friend reached in his brief case and took out a thin pamphlet and handed it to me; "Study that!" He said with a smile and a wink. It was a colored anatomy of the human body in overlaying cutout pages – put out by an American drug company. It was in English and only six or seven pages but it was beautiful . I was hooked. I could hardly wait for tomorrow to arrive.

In the hospital, my father's friend met me for a pep talk and instruction. "Medicine is an art," he said. "It is an art of listening, sensing, looking, and finally examining. Your grandmother is a master of this art. I will never be as good a doctor as she is!" He continued, "You don't know this, even *she* doesn't know this, but I have referred patients to her." He said with a smile and then laughed heartily at my shocked expression . My grandmother was a sort of medicine woman who had an immense knowledge of folk remedies but for all practical purposes was illiterate. A voice behind me broke into my surprise. I turned to see a rather large middle-aged lady in nurse uniform. I was introduced to a cantankerous woman with a mustache and wild wavy hair under a scarf. "This is Lady Mehri (not her real name), she is the Chief Nurse here." My benefactor whispered to me to follow her and listen to what she has to say. "She *too* is a master in the art of medicine!" he said and left us.

She was told to find me a job that would teach me something about medicine. She gave me one of those *if looks could kill* glances and grumbled her disapproval. She then grabbed me by the arm and with a most ominous hush voice said; "People around here are too busy to teach a little kid like you," she continued, "so *you* better not interfere with other workers and have them get behind in their work." I was overwhelmed by her demeanor and overpowering posture and thought that maybe I shouldn't be there.

She led me to the basement and down a long dark hallway to a hot steamy room. The name on the door said "Instrument Room." Several women were hard at work in that room and briefly looked up as we entered. I was shoved behind a rusty steel topped table with a large sink in the middle of it and somebody pointed to a basket full of strange looking tweezers, pliers and gadgets, and told me to start washing them. Before I had a chance to say anything or even introduce myself, I was soaked up to my elbows in strange smelling soapy water. In the corner of the room a huge drum with pipes attached to it sat hissing and belching like a steam locomotive. I learned that it was an autoclave and used to sterilize the instruments I washed.

Over the next couple of weeks, I was scolded numerous times about not getting all the blood, puss, and dead tissue out from within the teeth of those awful looking things and learned that they were *surgical instruments* each having a different name.

In fear of Old Hairy Face, I scrubbed, rinsed and cleaned those instruments until they shined. Cleaning the core of the needles was particularly challenging. God knows how many times I stabbed myself with them. It is a miracle that I did not get hepatitis. My hands were wrinkled beyond recognition and they ached at night – gloves were not used back then. Still I could not please her.

One day, by chance I was passing a patient's room and saw nurse Mehri tending to a young woman. I was shocked to see the tenderness and compassion with which she cared for that patient. Her manner was almost ministerial. I could not believe that kindness from someone who ran the place with an iron fist.

I kept washing, cleaning and sterilizing instruments but could not see what this had to do with me learning about medicine. So I went to confess to my doctor friend that I didn't like washing instruments.

"Who does?" He said, "It's a disgusting job cleaning all those germs, blood and crap from those instruments. But you want to be a brain surgeon, don't you?" He asked. "So first you have to learn all these instruments you are going to use. There is no better way to learn about them than washing, cleaning, and sterilizing them. After all, you don't expect *me* to wash them, do you?" he continued. "Because *I* did *my* instrument washing when *I* first started."

So it came to pass that I learned about needle types and sizes, hemostats, syringes, curettes, ring forceps, retractors, curved and long Kelly and many other instruments. The bossy nurse kept at me. Her fiery looks bore into my very soul and I learned quickly to follow orders. In fear of facing her wrath, I was all attention. Still I made all the usual mistakes and listened to many smirks of laughter behind my back. But in spite of everything that fearsome nurse mothered me to the understanding of all that matters in the world of caring for sick and injured. "The most important thing," she used to say; "is to listen to the patient."

Then one day my doctor benefactor called me into the operating room and asked, "Do you think that by now you know all those instruments?" I looked around at all the tables, lights and people in sterile attire and said, "Who, me?"

The moment of truth had arrived. Real shakes.

A real patient lay on the table. My benefactor – now instructor – guided me to the sink in the corner of the room and said to observe and follow his proper washing and scrubbing technique. With great trepidation I mirrored every move of his. When he was satisfied that I was clean, we walked on to a special mat to discharge all electricity from our body.

"We can't have any sparks in the OR," he explained. "The ether is explosive."

I nodded, as though I understood, not having a clue what he was talking about. *What is explosive?*

My head was spinning, my ears were having trouble adjusting to the sounds of hissing tubes, gyrating (ambo) bags and other noises, and a strange smell filled the room.

"If you feel dizzy let somebody know. It may be the *ether*."

A man in surgical scrubs (the scrub nurse) guided me to the back-side of a table full of instruments, neatly placed in rows. He put a gown on me and lightly tied my hands behind my back. "Don't touch anything. If you feel dizzy, you can pull your arms out from behind your back and sit down." I felt like sitting down, just then. Oh God, what if I faint and fall on the table, what if that thing explodes and I am killed, oh God, what if... But nothing happened.

Soon the patient was asleep, the anesthesiologist kept a cloth mask over his face and occasionally dripped ether over it. A strong noisy fan blew fresh air into the room, adding to the confusing racket. I never saw any of the procedure, itself. But every time the surgeon asked for an instrument, the scrub nurse looked at me and I was to point to it verbally and he handed it to the doctor. Halfway through the surgery, I started to feel confident and relaxed. I *knew* all the instruments. Hey, I can do this! I felt proud; this is easier than I thought. *NOT!!!*

Twenty minutes later – which felt like twenty hours – the appendectomy was over. The surgeon removed something from a small incision in the patient's abdomen and placed it into a basin held by the assistant and closed the little hole. All was over, but not for me. Over the next few days I told my heroic experience to family and friends over and over again. Every time, I repeated the story it got more dazzling. Before long my brothers and sisters were spreading the word around the neighborhood that *I* did the surgery and saved a man's life.

Back at the hospital, I continued to observe and work in the OR. Before long, I was passing instruments, which lead to collaboration with other assistants and finally assisting. Over the next three years, I assisted on many surgical cases and learned much about health and illness, until one day I left home for America.

Now, nearly sixty years later, my experiences include; practice in several countries on three continents, a military service in the United States Air Force Medical Corps during the Vietnam War era, work in rural as well as urban settings, teaching and serving on many medical boards and committees.

We have come a long way from the days of ether for anesthesia, re-usable syringes and needles, and rusted instruments. Yet we have a long way to go in order to incorporate all the new technology into our practice without losing the *Art of Medicine and Patientcare.*

HERE WE ARE

Over the past sixty years of working in the field of medicine, I have seen many changes, yet we are still struggling to bring needed healthcare to many people of our country and the world. The recent Coronavirus pandemic is a good example of how unprepared humanity is for such scourges of mother nature.

Today, medicine has become more technical than an art form. Patients fill their history and make their appointments online. Smart phones and computers take their vital signs and relay it to their electronic health records. Medical software identifies possible medications in conflict and suggests a differential diagnosis. The Internet, robotics, nano-technology and wireless communication are helping us be in many places at once and treat patients near and far.

All this technology should give us more time with our patients. Yet I find it disturbing that practitioners are forced to process patients rather than treat them. I have witnessed many who enter an exam-room, sit down and look at their laptop, question the patient, even examine the patient and walk out not knowing whom they saw, what the patient looked like or even if the patient was male or female.

I was working in a small resort town in Northern New Mexico a while back when a friend of mine at an orthopaedic clinic in a busy metropolitan city needed some time off, he asked me to go cover for him. There was a secondary reason for this invitation, however. My reputation had raised the curiosity of the physicians in that clinic, so they wanted to check me out and perhaps recruit me to join their practice. Since it was during off-season for me, I gladly accepted it. Once there however, the very busy practice and the rushed way of patient care became a turn off for me very quickly.

A particular incident killed the deal for good. One clinic rule was that all new providers were to present new injuries and fractures to the on-call physician before casting and discharging the patient (no problem there). On one very busy morning I saw a young patient with a non-displaced distal radius fracture. I informed the family that I was new and thus had to get my supervisor's OK before proceeding. They understood and after I informed the doc I was working with, we waited. The attending for that morning (a relatively young doctor who didn't know anything about me) had arrived late and was very busy seeing his own patients and so took a long time to get to me. But finally after multiple requests, he dashed into my room, walked to the viewing box, took a quick look at the x-rays, walked to the patient and made a cursory exam of the wrist and told me, "Put him in a short arm cast and let me see him back in 6 weeks." And without talking to the patient or the family, left the room. Now my custom was to re-check the cast in two weeks and change it. This is because once the swelling subsides, many casts loosen and also in the heat of that southwestern city, many children's casts become rancid with sweat and dirt. So I ran after him and asked whether we should re-check the cast in two weeks? He gave me an annoying look over his shoulder and snapped back that six weeks would be fine and if he had any problems he could just return and be seen in the walk-in clinic, and again rushed away from me. So I cried after him; "The family lives too far and the patient is a girl, not a boy!"

Good or bad, here we are. Still we need to remember that medicine is the art of caring for people. People with feelings, needs and problems. In this respect, we must assure our healthcare establishment to be a sanctuary, free of all political, social and racial bias and prejudice. Those who come to us must feel that their medical need is cared for and not be afraid of being further harmed. Our only objective should be to care for their healthcare need and be cognizant of the contributing factors and elements and not add to them.

GRAND-LADY

We may have the best medical system in the world but we also have some of the gravest problems. One of the most critical and costly is the opioid crisis. Fingers are pointed to many culprits. Maybe everyone is somehow at fault, or it may be that we are missing the true reason. I feel that one of the main causes for the problem is the lack of a true relationship between the practitioners and the patients. Practitioners are taught how to deal with diseases but not the patient.

Another problem adding to the confusion and complication of dealing with the dilemma is the individualistic nature of our society, as in many cases it has eliminated the cohesiveness of the family structure. Absence of older family members and their guidance leaves many younger people confused and uncertain on how to deal with their problems.

I lost my mother when I was two years old and was raised by my paternal grandmother. She was a sort of medicine woman who had an immense knowledge of folk remedies but for all practical purposes, illiterate. She was well known and had a large following.

Opium was legal back then in my country of birth. My grandmother used it extensively in her treatment of pain and discomfort. Not once did any of her patients become addicted to it because of her treatments. "For every day that someone takes it (opium), takes him two days to get off of it." She used to say. She always engaged the help of the patient's family before accepting to care for them. This was especially critical when she used pain medications of any kind.

Once an old and frail lady was brought to her. The elderly lady had fallen and dislocated her hip. The family lived in a rural village with no available transportation except donkeys and horses. The local healers tried without success to help her. As soon as she could tolerate the trip, she was taken to the nearest town, and then to a larger one and finally they arrived in the capital to see an orthopaedic surgeon. By then, some time had passed and they were told that her hip was frozen and she was too old and feeble to operate on. This was circa 1952 and surgical techniques and anesthesia was rudimentary at best, especially in the old Middle East.

After the old lady was turned away from all the specialists, someone had mentioned my grandmother to them and so they ended up at our doorstep. I was about eight years old at the time so I do not remember the details. But the process became the talk of the town for many years and Grand-lady , as my grandmother was called , talked to me about it many times afterward, mostly to answer my questions. Grand-lady entered into a long and challenging discussion with the family. Finally after numerous cups of tea, biscuits and promises, she agreed to take over her care with the understanding that no promises could be made since the injury was old and the patient elderly. She also confided that she accepted the case because the family had exhausted all options, and just could not return home with their relative untreated.

The family of the patient, her daughter and two grandsons (young adults), moved in with us. Grand-lady had the daughter prepare high energy soups, stews and drinks for our patient and instructed her boys to take turn massaging and rubbing their grandmother around the clock. She used warm oils, warm moist towels and mixture of home remedies in her massaging technique and administered small amounts of opium to ease the pain. She then sent my uncle to borrow a neighbor's small donkey. She tied the animal and placed a block of salt in front of it. The beast was allowed only a small amount of water.

By the nest day, the old patient had sufficiently relaxed, the donkey was crying for water and the boys were exhausted from massaging our patient. By this time the word had gotten around and many curious people wanted to know how the treatment was progressing. My father was furious and asked the local police to keep the nosy people at bay.

Finally Grand-lady felt the time was right, she gave the patient a healthy dose of opium and had the boys place her on the donkey. She then positioned the patient to her satisfaction and tied her legs together under the animal's belly and led it to a water trough. The boys continued their massage and Grand-lady started manipulating the patient's hip. The belly of the beast started swelling from all the water it was drinking and the distention supplied traction on the patient's leg and hips. The patient started yelling, the donkey kept drinking and Grand-lady shouted instruction while manipulating the hip. A loud pop in the hip momentarily silenced everyone before cries of joy and delight exploded in our house and then the neighborhood.

Years later Grand-lady conveyed to me that although the donkey provided a platform to anatomically align the patient's legs and hips, it was more for show and distraction than actual treatment. It provided enough diversion to allow her to do her manipulation without objection from the concerned family and observers.

Afterward, the family and especially the boys, were given strict and detailed instruction on how to provide physical therapy for the patient, continue the massage of her hips and legs for the next week or two and gradually withdrawing her from the opium. Grand-lady was of the opinion that the body healed itself, but if we injured it, then it is our responsibility to cure it. "And nothing" she used to say "damages a body more than alcohol and narcotics."

The grateful family returned home very happy and for years they sent us boxes of grapes, apples and other fruits as a token of their appreciation.

JANUARY

Of note in January:

Three days after graduating from high school, my father got me a passport, a one way ticket to NYC, gave me sixty dollars and said: "Come back a doctor."

I arrived in NYC, USA on Jan. 1, 1962 at about 11 PM in a snowstorm. I was 17 years old.

January 1, 1660 – Samuel Pepys started his diary of "Life in London." It included the Great Plague of 1664-65 and the Great Fire of 1666.

January 4, 1809 (1852) – Louis Braille was born in France. Blinded as a boy, he invented the Braille reading system for the blind using punch marks in paper.

January 8, 1964 – President Lyndon Johnson declared War on Poverty during his State of the Union address to the Congress.

January 11, 1964 – The U.S. Surgeon General declared cigarettes may be hazardous to your health.

January 14, 1875 (1965) – Philosopher-physician Albert Schweitzer was born in Upper Alsace, Germany. He served as a medical missionary in Africa and received the 1952 Nobel Peace Prize.

January 22, 1973 – The U.S. Supreme Court announced its decision in the case of *Roe vs. Wade* making abortion legal.

January 23, 1849 – Elizabeth Blackwell received her MD degree becoming America's first woman doctor.

NEW YEAR

On some New Year days, I stayed at home.

And on some, I've been far away.

Sometimes, far away places *were* home.

Other times, home; far away!

No matter where I was though, there were those who called it home! Celebrating the coming new year, wishing each other good health, prosperity and a resolve to be better in whatever they do. Though prosperity may be more *wishful thinking, good health* is what we all strive for. In illness, we pray for rapid recovery and hope to receive help fast. Help however, may come from unexpected and unusual places. To this, a sage healer remains wise and amenable.

Camping in the wilderness once, I observed a rather large injured lizard, chewing repeatedly on the bark of a tree by the stream. I was fascinated and curious, as I could not see any nutritional value in that bark. Years later, studying herbal medicine, I learned that the tree was a White Willow and its bark contained salicylic acid (aspirin). The lizard knew, as I did not, where to find medicine for its pain.

Through my many travels, I have learned that people approach problems according to the beliefs and customs of their land and time. Often, I interjected my Western learned knowledge to their true and proven remedy, only to find – to my surprise – for it to be inferior to what was practiced there.

Long ago, while working on a volcanic Caribbean island, I saw a young boy rubbing mud from a hot spring into a cut on his leg. I objected but was assured by him that it would help it heal. Over the following days I saw the boy several times and he would proudly show me his healing wound. Back at the clinic, I was told by the local doctor that the mud contained sulfur, iron and many other minerals. The acidic hot spring water thus acted as an antibiotic and had healing properties.

Today the power of our technology allows us to learn as well as teach one another around the world. There is so much knowledge that we can share for the betterment of ourselves and others. It is great that not only can we treat patients with our modern medicine, but also understand, know and learn their cultural and home remedies. For what makes home such a special place is that besides being a safe abode, it heals us of our ills by the knowledge local to it, and that is very precious. I, for one, see an immense opportunity in sharing the health of the world through these technological tools. But only if we keep an open mind and value others' knowledge as equal to ours.

OPIOID CRISIS

Today, the opioid crisis has become a dangerous epidemic in our world. The solutions offered by the so-called experts and the authorities are more problematic than curative. In a January 3, 2017 article in the *Boston Globe*, Felice J. Freyer wrote how; "Doctors are cutting opioids, even if it harms patients." In her article she iterated that; "Doctors face myriad pressures as they struggle to treat addiction and chronic pain, two complex conditions in which most physicians receive little training."

I find it astounding that an illiterate, self taught person like Grand-lady understood and knew how to use and discontinue opioids, but highly educated and experienced providers in today's world have no clue on how to deal with this dilemma. Grand-lady always enrolled a family member in the task of treating a patient. But when a patient shows up in our office alone, that option is not available. Our system is more apt to stigmatize these people than to treat them.

Walking to a subway station after a long day of work at a Methadone Clinic in Upper Manhattan in NYC, a long time ago, I heard the haunting voice of Esther Phillips sobbing over the radio. She was singing the song; *Home Is Where the Hatred Is* (written by Gil Scott-Heron – It can be heard on YouTube or you can search for it, it is well worth listening to). I froze in place, listening to the powerful and timely song. I felt my heart racing and a feeling of hopelessness filled my chest. The song tells of the bleakness of an addict's life and the unsympathetic reaction of our society to his/her predicament.

The work at the Methadone Clinic was a part of my internship of the PA/medical school I attended. The song accentuated the desperation of people I saw all day. My experience was exhausting and depressing. It was early 1970s and many young people were recovering from the sixties world of; *sex, drugs and rock & roll*. How so many did so much damage to their bodies in such a time was a testament to the broken society we lived in. In no place was this more prevalent than in the ghettos of American cities. (Ghettos of American cities – boy, talk about an oxymoronic statement.)

Many of the young were homeless, lived alone or in shelters that provided them an enclosure and nothing else. They were on probation or in hiding from family and authorities. Outside the methadone clinic, most had no support structure. Alone at home, with the nerve endings of their body firing like a shortened light bulb it was easy to see why they would reach for anything that would quiet the pain. Relapsed and back in our clinic, they would be criticized, stigmatized and ridiculed.

"These people need more help than a dose of methadone." I said once in protest.

"Well do you want to take them home and baby them?" Snapped an unsympathetic nurse working with me.

At the organization *AA*, an alcoholic seeking recovery is assigned a partner to help him or her stay clean. Now just think what a great idea it would be to insist on having a patient have a partner when we *start* him or her on an opioid regiment to prevent him getting hooked. The crisis would vanish.

RIKERS ISLAND PRISON HOSPITAL

My time at Rikers – not as an inmate, but rather as a healthcare provider – was fragmented and unsettling, yet insightful. New York City's Department of Health was responsible for providing healthcare personnel to the Rikers Island Hospital, a large, multi-story prison hospital.

One day, soon after I started my medical school training at US Public Health Hospital PA program in Staten Island, a couple of people from the NYC Dept. of Health showed up and announced that the City would be hiring any of us who would like to work for them after graduation and would start paying us right away. Well it didn't take much convincing for me to sign up. Especially once I found out that I could use the experience as part of my internship.

"Where will we be working?" was one of the first questions.

"The City has many Clinics in all the boroughs. You can have your choice."

Sounded too good to be true. *It was!* The clinics were the least desirable types of medical practice any of us entering a medical career would like to contemplate choosing. They included clinics for people with venereal diseases (VD Clinic), Tuberculosis (TB Clinic), Methadone Clinic for drug addicts and Prison Healthcare. Granted, many healthcare providers do work in these specialties and they are rewarding. As a matter of fact several of my classmates who did sign up in the program did stay in those fields, but I could not see it as the proper way to enter a career in medicine. Moreover, by the time I started PA/medical school, I had about 15 years of medical experience. My experience was mostly in surgical or emergency medicine and I wanted more training in those departments. So it was that a hospital experience sounded more desirable, even if it was in a prison system. Thus I chose to work at the Rikers Island Hospital. And Rikers was one place that I could work on the weekends and get extra pay for it. Still I had serious reservations after the first time I called to get information on how to get there and whom to see once there.

"Rikers Island, Officer Blood!" a harsh voice answered my call.

I was quiet for a bit. Is this a joke, is this guy's name really Blood?

"Hello, Officer Blood here,"

That *was* his name – how appropriate!

So after much soul searching I started working there one weekend a month.

The weekend job was more like being on call. I was to administer medication to chronically ill inmates and see urgent and critical cases. But in the prison system not much was considered urgent that needed immediate attention. So most of the time I just spent sitting there working on my homework. Occasionally skirmishes would happen and someone would need their injuries cared for.

Once I graduated medical school and entered a kind of internship however, I was permanently assigned to Rikers and a whole different type of practice opened up for me. One problem was that the hospital was dangerously understaffed with professional caregivers. Doctors were especially hard to find willing to work there. Most were like myself, working part time – while in medical school or residency – to make some extra money. I often found myself caring for a large population of inmates with special needs.

Rikers housed some notorious criminals. Some were wounded in their process of being arrested. A large number of Mafia members were among them – they were not nice. One particular Mafia Lieutenant was shot during his arrest and was paralyzed from the waist down. So he was a permanent resident of the hospital. While in prison, members of rival gangs or groups had injured him further with cuts and burns so he needed regular care. This man was vile and caring for him was challenging, to say the least.

Among the inmates were many young people who were there for minor infractions of the law. In my opinion, they did not belong with all the career criminals. Yet there they were. I would often have talks with them and encouraged them to go to school and get a new start in life. I am aghast at how many young people are in our prison system and how they are incarcerated with adults. As far as I am concerned, I think that people younger than 25 years old should be in a proper rehabilitation center, educated and released quickly and guaranteed a job.

My work at Rikers came to an abrupt end one day when I found out that I was one of only two providers there. All the doctors had resigned or finished their contract and they had not been replaced yet. I was expected to run a large part of the hospital by myself. The hospital also had a rather large psychiatric ward with many inmates in solitary confinement and being treated with questionable and strong sedatives and psychiatric drugs – some of which were experimental – and needed administering daily. They were prescribed by psychiatrists I didn't know who visited the place a couple of times a week. Legally speaking, I was still a student. I knew nothing about these drugs and refused to administer them for fear of getting sued by the inmates and ending up there as one of them. So to my relief and delight, I was fired. I could tell many tales and stories about what I saw and learned in my short time at Rikers but they would be out of the sphere of this book. I am relieved to learn that many improvements have been made to the healthcare system in our prisons all around the country. New technologies are helping; I just hope that these tools are not abused.

ARE WE READY?

In the protectionism environment of our world, the gap between prosperous and deprived keeps growing. In the past, such inequalities have sparked discontent that turned into raging fires of revolution and chaos. With every revolt, more people are displaced. With the increase of such masses, nations feel obliged to close their borders, strengthen fences and erect taller walls, leaving people in limbo and desperate, adding to the instability.

Albert Schweitzer, who was born on January 14, 1875 (–1965), winner of the 1952 Nobel Peace Prize, felt that a big problem of our history is the fact that after every war, the victors write the accounts of what happened and in doing so they also feel obliged to write new rules for the world to follow. This inherently sows the seeds of future conflicts. In his long and historic acceptance speech for the Nobel Peace Prize he said that after every war, the tragedy of displacing people from their homes and forcing them into exile was the most abhorrent human rights abuse. He goes on to state, "What really matters is that we should all of us realize that we are guilty of inhumanity." And the best way to overcome this is by working towards a world without war. After that award, Schweitzer spent the rest of his life working to abolish nuclear weapons and, unfortunately, was unsuccessful. However, we can learn from his example and though we may not be able to end all wars we can work to decrease inequalities and increase access to basic human rights such as health and education.

The biggest eye opener in the recent pandemic was just how unprepared the healthcare system is to deal with such potential threats. This was even more challenging when politicians politicized the problem. The recent

Covid-19 deadly disease was not a medical pandemic, it was a political one. The medical community could have got a handle on it much quicker were it not for all who tried to deny it, hide it, downplay it, blame it on others, and shun responsibility for it. As healthcare providers we are no more ready to deal with such a calamity than anyone else. In these times we must be immensely mindful of the welfare of our patients, especially when we are hampered by those who know nothing about the science of such diseases. Pandemics and such do not differentiate between people's race, religion, nationality or legal status. So it behooves us to think about such disparities and care for everyone well.

WHAT ONCE WAS

On January 11th in 1838 a telegraph message was sent using dots and dashes at Speedwell Ironworks, Morristown, New Jersey. Samuel Morse and Alfred Vail collaborated in developing the telegraph. The First Transcontinental Railroad (built between 1863 and 1869) and the Transcontinental Telegraph lines were built simultaneously. It was the telegraph that made communication between two points along the railroad possible and expedite the movement of needed supplies and information. It is interesting that their story is reported as a forgotten history by the Smithsonian. It shows how quickly we lose touch of our past in this fast moving world.

Recently going through some old photographs, I found an aerial picture I had taken of Embudo Hospital (now closed) that brought back many memories and confirms how fast our history is lost. Back at the turn of the last century, the Presbyterian Church was serving the medical needs of Northern New Mexico with missionary doctors and was planning to build a hospital in the town there. Legend has it that one evening, the local missionary doctor was called to help a woman having trouble giving birth and in distress. The woman's husband was at a friend's house drinking and upon return found out about the incident. In his drunken stupor, he became outraged that a strange man had looked at his wife – not withstanding the fact that he had been a physician and had helped deliver his child. The drunken husband found the doctor riding home on his horse and buggy and beat him mercilessly. After hearing the story, the church canceled the plan to build a hospital in that town and instead built it twenty miles away at the confluence of the Embudo River and the Rio Grande. For many years it was the only hospital north of Santa Fe.

In the early seventies, Presbyterian Medical Services (PMS) took over the administration of the hospital. Soon afterward federal grants became available for rural hospitals and PMS successfully bid and was granted a big chunk of money with which it also took over the running of the hospitals in the nearby towns of Española and Taos. I happened on the scene in 1974 just before PMS decided that with these new hospitals, the one in Embudo was not needed and closed it. With that, an important piece of Northern New Mexico history was closed. The outraged community organized a board and we turned the hospital building into a clinic, which operates to this day.

In 1975, I took my girlfriend to see the newly released movie; "The Great Waldo Pepper" about an aviator of the 1920s. The movie touched a nerve with me. I had started flying in 1969 while I was in the service, but after my discharge due to financial reasons, medical school, travels, etc. I stopped flying. Leaving the theater that night, I felt an elemental passion awaken in me and felt the need to start flying again. On the way home we drove to an airport and sat in the dark in an old aircraft tied down on the tarmac and fantasized flying it. The next week, I drove back to the Santa Fe Airport and signed up for flying refresher classes. Over the years, I went on to become a commercial pilot and have since flown to and from all kinds of places and seen many changes. Two of my favorite airports in NM have since closed and for the same reasons many rural hospitals have – urbanization of the wrong kind, financial burdens, and government regulation to name a few. Today I can only recall memories by looking at pictures I took with a camera I can no longer use (no film) of hospitals and airports that are all closed. What once was is gone, nothing that has replaced them even resembles them, like the cars that replaced the horse and buggy the missionary doctor rode to see his patients, digital cameras that have replaced my SLR, shopping malls that have replaced airports, and closed hospitals that are not renewed at all.

Perceptions and expectations of today's people look to futuristic types of solutions. In our field of healthcare; Telehealth, Telemedicine, and Tele-education are such tools and solutions. I don't know whether these advances are making us spiritually poorer or richer. But if there is one thing that I have learned in my journeys it is that our lives are molded, not by the knowledge that we gain but by the choices that me make! Let's hope our choices take us into a good future. Let's make sure that while we use these wonderful mechanisms, we stay in humane touch with those who come to us for help.

SOMETHING NEW

My coat didn't fit him well but it was warm. The evening chill was exaggerated by the brutal wind coming off the lake. Snow, blowing sideways seemed to go right through all the layers of clothing. January in Chicago can be brutal. Which makes one ask; why would anyone build a city here?

I was on leave from my military station in San Antonio, Texas. A friend - from Chicago - had ask me to accompany him home for the holidays and to meet his family. It was my first trip to the windy city and despite the warm reception, the beautiful holiday decorations and the food – oh boy, the food, after eating breakfast, lunch and dinner at the military mess hall for months, the home cooked meals were most appreciated – I still looked forward to returning to the warmth of Southern Texas.

New years are for new things, experiences and hopes. It was my first year in the service and I wanted to see as much of America and the world as possible. So I could not say no to an invitation to Chicago. Driving through a lot of Texas, Oklahoma, Missouri and Illinois gave me an appreciation of our country's size. Along the way, the many people representing many cultures, were too, an eye- opening experience. Maybe it was the holiday season but our encounters were warm, welcoming and friendly. It felt good to be welcomed. In Missouri, the chill hit me hard. I had not come prepared for that kind of cold. A sign on the highway informed us of a military base close by, so I decided to make a detour and visit the Post Exchange and pickup an overcoat. It was well used in Chicago.

Over the years of work and travel around the world, I have come to realize one thing about America that no other country can claim. No one can ever say that Americans all look alike! The diversity of our people is second to none and the power it gives us is unmatched. Although there are some who find our mixture threatening, I find it strengthening. For, what is beneath the skin of our bodies are souls with great ideologies, cultures, wisdom, intelligence and customs that profoundly congeal our strength as a nation.

My profession as a healthcare provider has been another key ingredient of my interaction with many people. It not only provided me with an adequate living but showed me the beauty of mankind, its humanity, civility, passion and yes, occasional brutality. No other profession can bring people intimately close so quickly. There is much wisdom to be gained from these encounters. None more enlightening than how universally everyone wants to stay healthy. This overwhelming desire of people helps keep us in business, yet it should not be taken for granted nor abused. This same need has helped the industry of healthcare to flourish. Today more money is spent in healthcare than most other businesses. New technologies further broaden our scope of practice but it should not isolate us from our patients. Rather it should help us get closer to more people and humanity. Still nothing compensates a human touch nor is more rewarding. Years later it is very likely that a tele-encounter will be forgotten but not a face to face act of kindness. Like the oversized coat I picked up in Missouri and gave to a homeless man in Chicago whom I found inadequately dressed fifty years ago.

FEBRUARY

Of note in February:

My First Child was born in February.

February 3rd, 1821 (1910) – The first female physician in the U.S., Elizabeth Blackwell was born near Bristol, England. She earned her MD from the Medical Institute of Geneva, New York, in 1849. She then established a hospital in New York City run by an all-female staff and trained women to be nurses in the American Civil War.

February is Black History Month. First recognized as such by American historian Carter G. Woodson, in 1926 as Black History Week. February is the birth month of President Abraham Lincoln (born February 12), who issued the Emancipation Proclamation, and black abolitionist, author, and orator Frederick Douglass (born February 14).

To honor the legacy of Lincoln and Douglass, Woodson chose February to celebrate their accomplishments as well as the history and achievements of black people in general. In 1976 President Gerald Ford officially recognized the month of February as Black History Month.

February 4, 1985 – Twenty countries signed the "Convention Against Torture and Other Cruel, Inhuman or Degrading Treatment or Punishment" document in the United Nations.

February 17, 1781 – The inventor of the stethoscope, French physician René Laennec was born in Brittany, France.

February 17, 1863 – The International Committee for Relief to the Wounded was established in Geneva, Switzerland, later to become the International Committee of the Red Cross.

BLACK HISTORY MONTH

One interesting thing about politics is that you never know whom you meet or when someone you know becomes truly important and famous. As one of the first PAs in New Mexico, I had my share of rubbing elbows with, arguing with, and even dancing with politicians. When I first moved to NM, not many people knew what a PA was and I had to fight to get recognized and eventually get licensed. But as destiny would have it, years later I ended holding the very job of the first person I met at the NM Board of Medical Examiners (later Medical Board) – who told me that NM does not recognize PAs and I would never practice in this state. Not only did we manage to get legislative approval, years later Governor Gary Johnson signed into law to allow PAs to serve on the Medical Board and I was the first PA appointed to that post by the next governor, Bill Richardson. The reason I am reminiscing this bit of history is to show how familiar we (PAs) are with people's unfairness and prejudices.

But back to meeting important people, when I served on the Medical Board we routinely attended the Federation of the State Medical Boards annual meetings. There we met and worked with representatives from other states and even countries. One such lady I had the honor to meet was Doctor Regina Benjamin from the Alabama Medical Board. Dr. Benjamin's history is most fascinating and enlightening. Born in Mobile, Alabama to a poor family, she had her share of tests and trials. In 1984, she was the first from her family to receive an M.D. She then worked as a clinician serving the fishing community of Bayou La Batre.

Dr. Benjamin became a true leader and was the first African-American woman and the first physician under age 40 to be elected to the American Medical Association's (AMA) board of trustees in 1995. She followed years later in 2002 with another big achievement, becoming the first black woman to lead a state-based medical society as president of the Medical Association of the State of Alabama. And still yet an even bigger achievement as the first African-American female physician to get appointed the U.S. 18th Surgeon General in 2009 – appointed by President Barack Obama.

Dr. Benjamin is now back at her La Batre clinic doing what she loves. Over the length of her career, she has received many honorary degrees and awards, including the Nelson Mandela Award for Health and Human Rights and the National Caring Award. So in this Black History Month, we take this opportunity to salute her and all African-American (and indeed all people of color) physicians, nurses and healthcare providers whose contribution cannot be overlooked or forgotten. Thank you!

African-American's role cover many aspects of our history. Most are not mentioned in any of our history books but should be memorialized as their contributions are as significant as those of any white person. Writers like Festus Claudius "Claude" McKay (Sept. 15, 1889 – May 22, 1948), a Jamaican writer and poet who was a central figure in the Harlem Renaissance and Gayl Jones (born Nov. 23, 1949), author of novels: Corregidora, Eva's Man, and The Healing.

And my favorite, Bessie Coleman – (Jan. 26,1892 – April 30,1926) the first black and Native American (her father was of Cherokee ancestry and her mother was African-American) female pilot.

Many more like Mae Jemison (10/17/1956) first black female astronaut, Dorothy Vaughan, Mary Jackson, and Miriam Mann whose contribution to computer sciences cannot be overstated. We salute them all!

PEOPLE ARE BEAUTIFUL

My daughter was showing me a Flash Mob performance of young musicians in Sao Paulo, Brazil on YouTube. The piece was Ravel's Bolero. The musicians were very young , high school age. Their performance was with such vigor, vitality, and enthusiasm that it filled my heart with joy. I was not familiar with the concept of Flash Mobs and became thrilled by it. I surfed around the Internet and found a few more fascinating performances. What I noticed the most however, was the goodness of the performers and the happiness they raised in the surprised and enthralled passer-bys. Not a face without a smile. It shows the goodness many bring to our world with so little effort.

This was noteworthy because I wrote this article in the month of February and Feb. 19 was the birthday of Lula Carson Smith who wrote under the penname of Carson McCullers, in Columbus, Georgia (1917). Author of *The heart is a lonely hunter* and many others. Although her writings were often of tragedies in people's lives, they equally portrayed the kindness of many others as well.

In *The Ballad of the Sad Café*, she wrote: "*The most outlandish people can be the stimulus for love. ...*

... The beloved may be treacherous, greasy-headed, and given to evil habits. ... but that does not affect the evolution of his love one whit. ... It is for this reason that most of us would rather love than be loved."

To love is to give selflessly. It is the rationale for many of us in choosing medicine as a vocation. We care and give, love and provide solace to those who seek our help. It is a satisfying service that gets more fulfilling with age.

Nowhere does this present itself better than in the heart of a country doctor. Where we know everyone by name and their relations. Where payment sometimes comes in the form of eggs, milk, and tortillas rather than cash. Even city folk may recompense you with such gifts.

While working in a small town in Northern New Mexico, I once took care of a fisherman – up from the city for the day. He hooked himself while fishing and sought my help. I removed the hook and got to know him a bit and gave him a ride to his car. He loved fishing and the Rio Grande Gorge, close to my clinic, was his favorite fishing hole. He asked if I liked trout – well "yes" was my response. For the next couple of years, every time he came up fishing, he dropped a few of his catch for me on his way back to the city. A simple fishhook removal provided me with fresh fish for a couple of years.

Today's uncertain politics and conflicts around the world generate many needy people. These disorders make even the most well intentioned provider hesitant to volunteer his or her services. Being a samaritan however means overlooking one's own safety, security or well-being. In such work do we find that people are beautiful even when they are sick, hurt, homeless and destitute.

DARWIN DAY

February 12, 1809 was Abraham Lincoln's birthday and also Charles Darwin's birthday. Two giants of history who set our world on a new course, different yet parallel in scope and enormity. While Lincoln's revolution forever changed our social outlook of humanity in our country, Darwin's theory altered the very understanding of our existence. Both concepts faced enormous opposition and resistance from many levels of society. The religious groups were some of the most outspoken and ardent on both fronts. While many spiritual groups supported Lincoln's anti-slavery stance, many more staunchly opposed Darwin.

Today, while we clearly support Lincoln and Darwin's ideologies, we have vastly different philosophies on how to incorporate one or both into our own lives. But philosophical or political ideologies aside, our modern technological wonders of communication give everyone the tools to find support for their point of view – whatever that may be.

Many of us in healthcare entered our profession with the same zeal and ideology of making a difference in people's lives as well as our own. We have had many revolutionaries and pioneers in our own world. Here are some *women medical pioneers* that you have probably never even heard of (its worthwhile to look them up):

Susan LaFlesche Picotte (1865–1915) – The first Native American in the United States to receive a medical degree as a doctor.

Rebecca Lee Crumpler (1831–1895) – The first Black woman to earn a medical degree in the United States.

Trota Of Salerno (11th Century) – She wrote many books on women's health and promoted cleanliness, a balanced diet, exercise, and avoidance of stress.

Jane Sharp (1641–1671) – Her book *the Whole Art of Midwifery Discovered*, published in 1671, was the first on the subject to be produced by an Englishwoman.

Mary Seacole (1805–1881) – A Jamaican healer, who faced unfairness and discrimination as a black woman when she tried to volunteer as a nurse during the Crimean War (1854–1856). When her offer of help was turned down by the British, she went to the Crimea on her own.

Elizabeth Blackwell (1821–1910) – The first woman in America to receive a medical degree.

Elizabeth Garrett Anderson (1836–1917) – The first woman in England to receive a medical degree.

Yoshioka Yayoi (1871–1959) – She was a physician and women's rights activist. She founded the first medical school for women in Japan.

And then there were all those countless men and women of medicine, curanderas, and folk medicine sorts, who, although having little to no western type education, nevertheless had enormous knowledge of botany, herbs and concoctions of all kinds. Their wisdom has contributed much to our knowledge of health and medicine.

Fortunately for us today, modern communication brings all this knowledge right into our home with a click of a computer key. By the same token, it can make heroes of many of us by allowing us to share our knowledge and expertise with people all around the world. Let us build bridges, share our knowledge and help those in need everywhere. In these chaotic political and social times of uncertainty, people's physical and mental health suffer greatly. They turn to us, the healthcare providers, for help. It is important that we don't allow our own prejudices and views interfere with our work. As the newly elected (2017) President of Germany; Frank-Walter Steinmeier said: "Let's be brave and not make politics with fear, because then we don't have to be afraid of the future."

OLYMPIAN'S OLYMPIANS

Healthcare providers who, like athletes strive to improve themselves to the level of an Olympian, give our profession the credibility it deserves. At the Olympics, the collective performance of the athletes is what makes it a world event, but it must be remembered that it is the contestants' training and work that has earned them their place on the world stage, a tribute to the tenacity and resolve of their dream and vision.

The Olympics are one place where peace and harmony is demanded and permeates the very essence of the venue. It is where friend and foe gather to prove their mettle. History has proven that the process can also heal differences and create peace among adversaries. Indeed the tradition of the Olympic Truce or "Ekecheiria" dates back to the 9th century BC (its worthwhile to look this up). During the Truce period, the athletes, their support teams and families, as well as spectators, could travel in total safety to the Olympic games and return home. As the opening of the games approached, the sacred truce was proclaimed and announced by citizens of Elis who traveled throughout Greece to pass on the message.

Recently, the International Olympic Committee (IOC) decided to revive the ancient concept of the Olympic Truce to encourage searching for peaceful and diplomatic solutions to the conflicts around the world and to create a window of opportunity for dialogue and understanding.

In that respect, watching the Special Olympics is of great satisfaction when we see the marvelous achievements of the competitors. How they overcome their handicaps, shortcomings and limitations. Here too healthcare and medical technology often play a great role. Much of what is achievable today is due to breakthroughs in the healthcare devices. Advances in many areas help determine whether athletes reach their goals, ambitions and aspiration. People like Beatrice Vio – an Italian fencer with no arms, or Junichi Kawai a Japanese blind swimmer, or Chantal Petitclerc a Canadian wheelchair track athlete, Matt Stutzman of Fairfield, Iowa who is an armless champion archer, and how about Jessica Cox of Arizona, the first licensed armless pilot and many others; Olympians all.

In healthcare, too, we have Para Olympian caliber practitioners like; Dr. Gregory Snyder a physician in wheelchair, or Dr. Judith Ann Pachciarz who is deaf, or Dr. Cheri Blauwet who is an MD *and* a Para Olympian, or Dr. Tim Cordes who is blind. They are all inspirations to the rest of us. A long time ago I had an opportunity to work with a doctor who was a polio victim and in wheelchair. In my young and ignorant way, I did not quite appreciate him at first. As a matter of fact we used to give him difficult patients because they would pacify once they saw that their provider had more of a handicap than they. But over time I came to truly appreciate him and learned much about dealing with adversity. Handicapped healthcare providers are everywhere around the world. In many developing countries children with disabilities often become healthcare providers as they grow up. Many learn on the job to care for their friends and relatives with similar disabilities. Not all are educated by our western standard, yet the care they provide is invaluable and very much welcomed.

We might chuckle at the notion of the blind leading the blind but I have witnessed it first hand. Working in a rural, mountainous community sometime ago, I cared for a genetically deaf family. They lived in an isolated small canyon across the river. The bridge to their property could be described as rickety at best. The old pickup truck they used for transportation was in poor repair. Many in the community helped them but it was not enough. The first time I saw one of the family members, I was informed by our nurse of their condition. She asked me if I could do any follow ups as a home visit, since the family wouldn't ask themselves. A teenage family member had a rather large pilonidal cyst needing frequent I & D.

They were one of the most gracious and courteous families, I ever cared for. It took much convincing by our nurse – who knew a bit of sign language – and myself to allow me to go to their house and care for their daughter. A few days later our nurse lead me to their home. We parked on our side of the river and walked over the old wooden bridge. I couldn't believe that they would drive over that dilapidated crossing – but they did. Half way across the bridge, we could hear music playing. As we got closer, the music got louder and sounded eerie. By the time we got to the door we realized that their dog was howling to the music which made it sound eerie.

We were laughing when we entered and had to explain that we were laughing at the dog and not them. The mother who home schooled her family explained that music was a part of the home education curriculum package they had received in the mail. Although they could not hear the music, they could feel the vibration and differentiate the types and forms of it. I felt humble, as they seemed to understand and appreciate music more than I did.

Humanity demands caring for others and often it becomes a Herculean task for the caregiver and receiver. So as we watch many of these Olympian's Olympians, we must be thankful for all they teach us in adversity and be appreciative for all that we do not have to endure to do our job. Maybe then we can have a better outlook on our daily chores.

HEALTHCARE AND OUR LEGAL SYSTEM

Among the stack of mail on my desk was a letter from New Mexico (NM) Medical Review Commission asking me to serve on a hearing of an alleged malpractice case. The Commission was established by the NM legislature to provide hearings for potential malpractice cases against healthcare providers before they go to court. It consists of three providers and three attorneys sitting on the hearing where a patient and his or her lawyer are accusing a provider of negligent, wrongdoing or malpractice that has allegedly caused harm to that patient. On the other side, the provider and his or her attorney present their case, defending themselves. The majority of the cases arise from simple misunderstandings.

This experience along with my time served on the Medical Board has taught me much about the intricacies of the legal aspects of providing healthcare. While there are a few bad apples among us, I have found that overall my colleagues do an admirable job.

Although most hearings are straight forward, some are interesting for being utterly preposterous. Others may be classified as down right stupid and some, hilarious. There was a case a few years ago, where a patient had surgery by a very reputable surgeon. The outcome was not perfect due to the fact that the patient – an alcoholic – repeatedly damaged the surgical site. The surgeon and staff at that practice attended to that patient many more times than was needed to assure success of the case and they were successful in doing so despite the patient's total lack of concern. An attorney brought suite against the doctor claiming the doctor should have done a better job, as the patient's result was not optimal. But could not show what 'optimal' in such a case was nor did he even know anything about the case. The patient was not helpful either as it was obvious that it was past drink time.

On another case a patient, while visiting friends in a nearby town, shot himself in the leg by accident and was seen at the ER and cared for. On return home, did not seek follow up as he was supposed to. A few days later he developed chest pain and went to see his primary care provider (PCP) but did not mention the accidental gunshot wound to his leg. Many laboratory tests did not reveal what the history could have told the PCP. Lack of history and normal lab tests lead the PCP to treat him for a possible bronchial infection. The next day when his condition worsened, he refused hospitalization and still did not reveal the gunshot wound to his leg. The following day an embolism killed him so his wife sued the PCP for negligence and malpractice. At the hearing we asked the wife if she was present at the visits and she said yes. "Did your husband tell your PCP about the gunshot wound?" No! Was the answer. "Did *you* tell the PCP about it?" again no was the answer.

"Why not?"

"We didn't think that the two were related and my husband was embarrassed for shooting himself in the leg."

Right or wrong, our society allows for lawsuits, frivolous or not. As political atmosphere in our country turns, the chaos it creates could cause confusion that may lead to misunderstandings. Such misconceptions lead to lawsuits. Managed care organizations and insurance companies often settle with plaintiffs, as they find it cheaper than a prolonged trial. Unscrupulous attorneys find this beneficial, which adds to our dilemma. As providers, we must be alert to these conditions and protect ourselves as well as our patients. I recall an attorney friend jokingly tell me: *There are two kinds of doctors, those who have been sued and those who are going to be sued.*

UNEXPLAINED FEVER

I was working at the local university's student health center in the 1970s, when one evening, a female African-American student presented there with the complaint of general illness and high fever. I quickly realized that something was very wrong with this young lady. She looked quite ill and initial vital signs revealed a rapid pulse and 104°F fever.

The student claimed that she had gone camping a couple of weeks ago when she was visiting her family in the Midwest and since then had been feeling weak. But nothing serious till today, when she woke feeling lethargic with a slight bellyache. She went to class but the light bothered her eyes too much so she went back to her dorm room and slept. When her roommate came home after classes, she found her delirious and sweaty and brought her to the health center.

A call to the ER at the university hospital was made and the busy ER attendant notified. An ambulance was called, IV started, and she was transferred to the hospital.

I called the ER before leaving work at 11 PM and was told that the patient was admitted to the ICU and that "No, they didn't know what was wrong with her."

Overnight the condition of the young woman worsened. A team of internists and medical students made the early rounds and a new treatment regiment ordered. By late morning however, the patient's temperature spiked to 107°F and she passed away that afternoon.

The subsequent autopsy was not conclusive and a diagnosis of Q fever vs. acute liver failure was reported. Although Q fever was identified in 1930s, it was not well known or understood and the drug of choice to treat it; Doxycyline was relatively new (in 1970). Still, it did not exactly fit the symptoms either. What truly contributed to this patient's demise however was the lack of availability of accurate information, even at a university setting. Years later in the mid 1980s we discovered Human Monocytic Ehrlichiosis, a tick transmitted disease. The disease usually shows up in people with recent tick bites – which she may have contracted while camping with her family. The symptoms are typically high fever, abnormal hematology, elevated liver enzymes, and extreme light sensitivity. All of which were present in this young girl. Although most cases respond well to treatment, there have been fatalities and this may have been one.

To this day, I am saddened by the loss of that young lady. Although everything that could be done was done for her according to the knowledge of the time, we still lost her. Sometimes we just need to look deeper, question more, and be a detective in our search for answers. Today's communication technology should make it easier to research needed information, yet we still hear about missed diagnoses and wrong treatments to the detriment of patients. Today's rushed system of moneymaking practices do not help. We can do better.

SCIENCE AND HEALTHCARE

February 16, 1766 was the birthday of economist Thomas Robert Malthus, born in Surrey, England. In 1798, he published a pamphlet called "*An Essay on the Principle of Population*" in which he argued that the human population of the earth was growing at a faster rate than the food supply, and that war, disease, and famine along with abortion, birth control, prostitution, postponement of marriage and celibacy were necessary in order to prevent overpopulation.

More recently, Michael A. Morrisey of the University of Alabama wrote an article on the economics of healthcare where he argued that the economy of healthcare is different in that the outcomes are uncertain and that large segments of the industry are dominated by nonprofit providers and payments are made by third parties such as the government and private insurers making health care unique.

While the above predictions and observations may be true and correct, the fact remains that our population is growing rapidly and along with climate change resulting in environmental variants. The ever-changing population demography further creates challenges that healthcare providers have to deal with. While economically, it may be reasonable to accept the above scenarios as the basis of a problem our world is facing, finding a solution to them is our challenge.

It is also interesting to note that February 15, 1564, was the birthday of scientist Galileo Galilei, born in Pisa, Italy, who defended the scientific belief and prophesied that, in the future, "There will be opened a gateway and a road to a large and excellent science into which minds more piercing than mine shall penetrate to recesses still deeper." Galileo also said, "In questions of science, the authority of a thousand is not worth the humble reasoning of a single individual."

It is further interesting that Vatican scorned and even threaten him so much so that he publicly redacted some of his statements in order to be able to continue his work. Although the scientific community proved many of his theories and over the years, his discipline became the cornerstone of numerous other discoveries, the Vatican did not attest to its legitimacy until 1992 (some 350 years later). Which proves that ideologies for or against certain beliefs, values and ways of thinking can continue for years or centuries even in the face of undisputed evidence. Much like those who still believe that the world is flat. As healthcare providers we need to be aware of such thinking, not so much to argue about them but rather be alert of their potential contribution to a patient's particular problem.

Today Galileo's gateway has been discovered. Internet and telecommunication can help to expand healthcare to every corner of the globe, and provide expertise for all rare and strange maladies. Still this technology is new, so it is up to us to make the economists and politicians see the benefits of it.

THE CUSP OF CHANGE

Our world is changing. What comes out of this change will have profound ramifications on tomorrow's world. Historically major changes, as we witness now were done in limited or smaller arenas. Even in major conflicts like World Wars I and II, Korea, Vietnam etc. it took days for news from home to reach us in the form of a newspaper or newsreel. But today all around the world, we can witness the news from back home instantly even watch our family eat dinner or join family celebrations of all kinds on our smart phones.

In no time in history has mankind witnessed global changes and even participated in it as we do today. At the time of this writing for example, the evening news informs us of political upheaval in the Maldives, the coalition agreement reached in Germany's four month old elected government, the new offensive of the Turkish military forces against the Kurds, the unity of the North and South Korean Olympiads, the new government in Liberia, the mass migration of the northern South American population to Brazil, etc., etc.

Today's technology also reveals the many prejudices of history. Often history is written by the victors at the expense of the losers. But even when there are no clear sides, history tends to be selective about what was the story behind some major changes. The month of February is a good example of all that we celebrate and that which we don't. For example we celebrate Presidents Day in honor of George Washington and Abraham Lincoln. But two other presidents were also born in February; William Henry Harrison on Feb. 9, 1773 and Ronald Reagan on Feb. 6, 1911.

Of the twenty seven Constitutional Amendments, six of them were ratified in February. Speaking of Constitutional Amendments, one may ask, "*If* we are so proud of our Constitution, why the Amendments?" The answer of course is that the Constitution served the people of its time, but as time changes, the new needs of the people demand changes to it. The changes did not make it better or worse, rather it just met the demands of the time.

Another very good example of what has changed is the Boy Scouts of America. On February 8, 1910, the Boy Scouts of America was established. The Boy Scouts began as a movement in England in the early 20th century. William D. Boyce founded the Boy Scouts of America soon after as a way to keep young men (as the Scout Oath puts it) "physically strong, mentally awake and morally straight." What is moral today would not even be fathomed a hundred years ago. The evolution of how the Boy Scouts are practiced are a testimony to the changes that are controlling our society today.

In no place does change affect the people as it does in healthcare. We – the providers of healthcare – should be aware and have a direct input on any changes made to our delivery system. For, after all the arguments are made and rhetoric shouted across the aisles, laws are passed and politicians move on to other matters, we are still left to implement those changes and care for our patients. And if the new rules create more of a hindrance than help, it will be on our shoulders.

Fortunately for us, the new communication technology makes it easy for us to express our opinions and have our voices heard. But they need to hear our voices. The more of us speak up, the louder our voices will be. Please let's stay alert to what is coming our way. Let organizations such as American Medical Association (AMA), American Telemedicine Association (ATA), American Osteopathic Association (AOA), American Nurses Association (ANA), other professional organizations, and our state and local chapters hear our concerns. Help them make changes that we can live with, for the benefit of our patients and ourselves!

MARCH

Of Note in March

March 1, 1961 – President John F. Kennedy established the Peace Corps, an organization sending American volunteers to developing countries to assist with health care, education and other basic human needs.

March 10, 1880 – The Salvation Army was founded in the United States. The social service organization was founded in England by William Booth and today operates in 90 countries.

March 11, 1918 – The 'Spanish' influenza reached America as 107 soldiers became sick at Fort Riley, Kansas. Eventually a quarter of the U.S. population contracted the deadly virus, resulting in 500,000 deaths. By the end of 1920, the worldwide death toll approached 22 to 28 million.

March 11, 2020 – The World Health Organization declares the COVID-19 outbreak a pandemic.

March 14, 1833 (1910) – The first female dentist, Lucy Hobbs was born in New York. She received her degree in 1866 from the Ohio College of Dental Surgery and was a women's rights advocate.

March 14, 1879 (1955) – Albert Einstein was born in Ulm, Germany. His theory of relativity led to new ways of thinking about time, space, matter and energy. He received a Nobel Prize in 1921 and emigrated to the U.S. in 1933 where he was an outspoken critic of Nazi Germany. Believing the Nazis might develop an atomic bomb, he warned President Roosevelt and urged the development of the U.S. Atomic bomb.

March 19, 1813 (1873) – Explorer and medical missionary David Livingstone was born in Blantyre, Scotland. He arrived at Cape Town, Africa, in 1841 and began extensive missionary explorations, often traveling into areas that had never seen a white man. In his later years, he sought the source of the Nile River. He also became the subject of the famous search by news correspondent Henry Stanley who located him in 1871 near Lake Tanganyika in Africa after a difficult search and simply asked, "Dr. Livingstone, I presume?"

March 20, 1904 (1990) – American psychologist B.F. Skinner was born in Susquehanna, Pennsylvania. He pioneered theories of behaviorism and developed the Skinner box, a controlled environment for studying behavior.

March 21st – Spring Equinox – Spring begins – many cultures in the world celebrate this day as New Year.

March 31, 1933 – The Civilian Conservation Corps, the CCC, was founded. Unemployed men and youth were organized into quasi-military formations and worked outdoors in national parks and forests.

MUDDY SHOES

Poet Robert Frost was born in San Francisco in March of 1874. He was a farmer before becoming a famous poet. He said; "When I took a trip to New York City to try to interest editors in my poems, I was too much of a farmer, I had mud on my shoes. They could see the mud, and that didn't seem right to them for a poet."

In 1911 he sold his farm and moved to England. Several months after arriving in England, Frost published A Boy's Will (1913) and then North of Boston (1914), which sold 20,000 copies and made him famous. Frost won the Pulitzer Prize for poetry four times. He said, "In three words I can sum up everything I've learned about life: *It Goes On.*"

As it was with Frost's muddy shoes, people's expectations are based on their perceptions. Our patient's expectations demand that we help their lives go on healthily and painlessly. Even if that is not possible, if we give them the impression that we care about their well-being, it will ease their pain. Often, that can be done by just listening to them. The good Lord has given us one mouth but two ears. If we listen twice as much as we talk, we will make our patients very happy.

ONE AMONG THE MANY

Her name, I cannot recall, she, I will never forget. She was a mother of three fatherless boys. The boys were young, oldest only 6. The hardship of life was very present on her young tired face. Her genteel spirit and simple heart had been abused and she couldn't understand why she was where she was. Despite her depression, she was mothering her children well. I was treating her for asthma. She had an advanced and uncontrolled case of the disease. One that required frequent visits to the ER, sometimes daily.

I was working at a very busy emergency room in South Bronx, NY as part of my internship. It was one of the busiest in the city, state and perhaps the country. She would sit there holding a nebulizer to her face, breathing an aerosolized bronchodilator mixer. Watching her neighbors and locals come through the doors in all sorts of crisis added to her despair. Often, her three young and active boys played under her chair or nearby – being boys and causing havoc. The strain of the disease and her inability to cope with it and the life she was leading was wasting her away rapidly. I felt an incredible feeling of inadequacy, powerlessness and impotence. But had no solution, as did none of the other providers, caring for her. One very hot, busy summer night, her call for an ambulance was not answered in time. I did not see her again. Weeks later, I saw a neighbor of hers who occasionally would bring her to the ER and learned that she had had a severe attack and could not get help in time and passed away – while her children watched.

Unfortunately, for those of us who have worked in such places, these types of stories are common. While we strive to help and save our patients, we do lose some. It is the nature of our work. It is however, those whom we lose under circumstances beyond our control and conditions, which should not have been, that leave deep scars in the depths of our memory.

Looking back, we wonder how could it have been different. Retrospectively, we may have many solutions, anecdotes and *could have done thats* but the lessons we learned and can now pass on to our disciples are what matters. Our system can do better.

SPRING WINDS

Spring (spring equinox) arrives in the northern hemisphere around March 20th or 21st. Curious thing, seasons, how the spherical position and tilt of a planet can have such a profound effect on everything living. And how the same orientation has an opposite outcome on the other side of our globe. A few degrees of geometrical or geothermal change can influence our very existence. It is said that, "as the seasons form a great circle in their changing, so does the life of a person - from childhood to childhood." The spring winds are an integral driver of this circle and their stimulating powers too, bring new messages to the awaken; "Arise and start anew, for much awaits to be done. All things evolve from the creator and all must revolve to complete the circle of life!"

It is no wonder that many cultures celebrate this time as the start of their calendar year. It is not a religious celebration; rather it is a natural and cultural one of nature's annual beginning. In the zodiac, the astrological year begins as we enter the sign of Aries, which is around March 21st. Nurooz, which means new day, is still celebrated in Iran, Turkey, Pakistan and Afghanistan. Zoroastrians were one of the early cultures that started their year thus. It is a time of purification and setting one's intention for a new start. Even the western world celebrated spring as the New Year till Julius Caesar changed it to January in 45 BC.

The Mayan Culture too celebrated the spring equinox for hundreds of years before the Spanish arrived. The pyramid at Chichen Itza on the Yucatan Peninsula puts on quite a show on the occasion. Built around 1000 years ago, the pyramid is designed to cast a shadow on the equinox, outlining the body of Kukulkan, a feathered snake god. A serpent-head statue is located at the bottom of the pyramid, and as the sun sets on the day of the equinox, the sunlight and shadow show the body of the serpent joining with the head.

As people everywhere celebrate the coming of the spring, they wish each other health and prosperity. Yet in many parts of the world this is only wishful thinking and a hope. Even in this technologically advanced world of the twenty first century many live in squalid and inhumane conditions. Children grow up playing in running cesspools and breathe acrid air of industrial residue. The overwhelming exodus of many from their distressed surroundings is overpowering the resources of what used to be sanctuaries. Unfortunately, the future is unclear for refugees and asylum seekers. Such uncertainties distress people to mental instabilities and illness. According to the United Nation's World Health Organization; more than twelve million die every year due to unhealthy environments. From Dacca to Maseru, from La Paz to Mexico City and even in our own country from native reservations to Appalachian towns, many suffer the lack of proper sanitation and access to healthcare. Where are human rights, how can we help those in need, how can we make a difference?

To borrow Beyonce's wonderful and heart warming song; "I Was Here," by Diane Eve Warren sung at The United Nations' World Humanitarian Day on August 19, 2012: *How can we (as healthcare professionals) leave this world so others think kindly of us and remember our contribution to their health and well-being. That we made their "world a little better just because [we were] here!"* (It's worthwhile to look the original song up and listen to it.)

Today, this is easier than we think. Technology gives us the tools to make a difference, to touch people's lives, to bring some happiness to people in need. Let's make a difference!

HALLEY'S COMET &
THE WEST TEXAS SKIES

In May of the year 240 B.C.E., Chinese astronomers: Shih Chi and Wen Hsien Thung Khao noted the earliest recorded sighting of a comet that came to be known as Halley's comet. In the 18th century, the English astronomer Edmond Halley speculated that the comets seen in 1531, 1607, and 1682 were actually the same comet, returning at regular intervals. He predicted its return on Christmas Day of 1758. It did, but Halley didn't live to see it.

The Babylonian clay tablets recorded it in 164 B.C.E. and 87 B.C.E. It appeared in 1835, the year Mark Twain was born. In 1909, he said: "I came in with Halley's comet in 1835. It is coming again next year, and I expect to go out with it." He died on April 21, 1910, one day after the comet reached perihelion.

In March 1986, it returned again. Its returning cycle was significant to me as midlife crisis, family issues and financial struggles were causing chaos in my life and in one way or another, I felt the heavenly body might be responsible for them. Though it might have seemed superstitious, my human nature needed to blame something other than myself to sooth my distress.

Although its time of return was now well known and had been predicted well in advance, its orbit placed it too high to be seen well specially in a lighted city or surroundings. Its location in the night sky made it appear in the early hours of the morning in the northern hemisphere – another deterrent to look for it.

I was living in Lubbock, Texas at the time and was determined to see it. The first night, I drove as far out of the city as I could, but the comet was too dim and the lights of the many small towns in West Texas barred its visualization. Resolved to see it at all cost, I borrowed the Cessna aircraft of a friend and took to the sky about two AM, the following night. There were no clouds and I headed East over the Caprock breaks to a dark area and despite the big moon was able to locate the wanderer of our solar system low in the horizon. I was alone flying in the dark of that night gazing at Halley's comet, meditating and praying. On its previous visit to our neighborhood, aircrafts were not available to the average man. The fact that I was flying along with it seemed in itself futuristic and I wondered if mankind would be flying alongside of it in a spaceship on its next visit in 2061. The engine noise was a distraction and for a brief moment I considered shutting the engine and soaring in silence for a while but a glance at the menacing darkness below, changed my mind. The experience was sacred and spiritual.

The regularity of events in our universe and many ways in my own life had me reflecting on all that destiny throws at us. The many cycles of nature and how they affect, even control our very existence. Halley's comet's appearance reveals one such cycle of many things in nature. Though we have learned to accept and realize many of these heavenly cycles, we do not readily accept the cycle of many other occurrences in our own world; the cycles of poverty, war, famine, natural calamities, diseases, etc. Their cause and effect should be clear and obvious, yet the order of our world today proves otherwise. Comets have been associated with good and bad luck. In 1986 there was no useable Internet, but by the time Comet Hyakutake appeared in March 1996, we were routinely using it. Today this technology is creating unmatched opportunities, both good and bad. What we need now is the wisdom to use it to our advantage and in a good way.

ANDRE RIEU

Andre Rieu is a world renowned conductor/ musician who has been successful because on his tours he brings in local and unknown musicians and involves the audience in his performances and makes them happy. Even when he plays gloomy songs and music.

In making music happy, even when it's not, one must understand humanity. No one appreciates or wants sorrow. So when facing pain, any relief is welcomed, even a momentary and false one.

In no place is this more important and necessary than in healthcare. Pain is a presence in life that we have to deal with. In the old days, families were close and comforted each other in such times. Today we use medications such as opioids, marijuana, etc. and when our patients get hooked, we blame them and accuse them of being drug seekers and addicts. Perhaps we should have helped them deal with their pain in other ways than with drugs.

A friend once told me that on a trip overseas he was walking by a river and saw gypsies dancing under a bridge. Joyous, he walked down to join the festivities only to find that he had entered a funeral procession. A depression overtook him and he found the contradictory atmosphere of the scene confusing, yet it had a soothing and relaxing quality that reduced the grief of the mourners.

Today's business of medicine is not conducive to such approaches. For-profit healthcare requires processing people rather than spending time to find the root of their problem. This is especially true in our rural communities with limited access to healthcare. Many rural hospitals are closing because they are not profitable. We must remember however that these hospitals were not built to be profitable, rather to serve their community. But new communication tools can help guide many toward alternatives; such as music, meditation, prayer, dance, physical activity, community involvement (as Rieu does) and many other useful and safe methods. Let's embrace this technology and through it bring hope and help to our citizens near and far.

WOMEN'S DAY

March 8th is the International Women's Day. Congratulations to all the women in the world, in business, politics, science, education, medicine, engineering, aerospace, and all the other fields that their contributions have been important. But I would like to also recognize all the selfless ladies whose tireless work supports the very fabric of families and societies. The nuns and ladies of many persuasions who run shelters and clinics in very rural and desolate areas of the world. The volunteer nurses and doctors who feel more rewarded helping the needy in the ghettoes or war torn regions of the world than working in a plush urban hospital. The female members of many societies who face the daily barrage of harassment in order to provide for their families. *They* are the real heroes in my book.

People like; Idawalley Zorada Lewis Wilson (Born February 25, 1842 – 1911), an American lighthouse keeper in Newport, Rhode Island. She is noted for her heroism in rescuing people from the sea. On July 16, 1881, she was awarded the prestigious, Gold Lifesaving Medal.

Today there is an Ida Lewis Light house, an Ida Lewis yacht Club and museum and at least two pieces of music were named for her: the Ida Lewis Waltz, and the Rescue Polka Mazurka. There is even a Coast Guard ship named after her.

And Grace Hopper (Born December 9, 1906). She received a Ph.D. in mathematics from Yale. During World War II, she joined the Navy and was assigned to work on a machine calculating rocket trajectories. In 1950s she worked on some of the original computers and wrote one of the first programs that used ordinary language – known as COBOL, or "Common Business-Oriented Language."

In medicine and healthcare too we see many heroic women devoting their lives to serve others. Working in a small town in rural Colorado, a long time ago, I had the privilege of practicing alongside a wonderful nun and nurse whose name (unfortunately) I cannot recall – let's call her Sister Patrice for this narrative. She and several other nuns traveled from a rectory in Walsenburg, CO. They would attend to the people living in isolation in the Southern Colorado Mountains, many of whom were handicapped by age, genetic problems, illness, or other maladies. Although all these care-givers were wonderful in their devotion, my colleague was truly noble in her efforts. She would drive many miles on the mountainous and dangerous roads of the area to deliver care to people who at times were not even aware of her presence. In winter, those roads were particularly treacherous, but that would not deter her. I learned a lot from that lady, particularly obstetrics, as I helped her deliver several children. Some of the deliveries were under extremely trying conditions, as many families lived in primitive conditions without electricity or proper plumbing.

I recall a particular case the day after a stormy and snowy Thanksgiving. We got a call on the radio that one of Sister Patrice's pregnant ladies was in labor. I volunteered to go with her and drove her 4 wheel drive car to an isolated village in the mountains. The snowy road was very slippery and I was having some trouble negotiating it. Coming on to a particularly steep curve, she mentioned and I heard it a bit too late that that bend was a bad one and skid into the side of the hill and got stuck. I jumped out to investigate and ran back to ask her for help, only to see her disappear into the storm, carrying her OB bag and rushing on in the ankle deep snow. Surprised, I stood there baffled and uncertain as what to do. I was about to run after her when the local sheriff happened by. He had heard the same call and was on his way and was surprised that we had beat him. He stopped and I asked him to find Sister Patrice and take her to her destination. He did and came back to help me.

By the time we reached the new mother's small and dark house, Sister Patrice had delivered the baby and was attending to the mother. There were several other ladies at hand and helping. When Sister Patrice saw me, smiled and said; *it's a boy.* She then proceeded to show me a small tear on the mother's vagina lip and asked me to suture it close. As I was attending to my work, I noticed Sister Patrice walking barefoot.

"What happened to your shoes?" I asked.

"Oh, they were full of snow, so I took them off." Was her selfless and undaunted answer.

It is noteworthy that in those days long distanced communication was not easily available. Our small clinic was sixty miles from the nearest town and any semblance of a hospital (twelve beds, one doctor and another part time physician visiting from the nearest city 120 miles away). To make a long distance phone call, we dialed the operator and gave her the number we were trying to reach and then waited for the operator to contact that hospital, university or specialist and have them call us back. Sometimes we would not even hear from them for a day or two. Today the modern communication technology allows us almost immediate access to specialists anywhere. High quality cameras – even in our cell phones – eliminates the need of tediously describing many patient's conditions verbally.

Although these incredible technologies put us in closer contact, many of our citizens still live in isolation throughout the world and many health-care providers – women and men – still care for them with a great deal of difficulty. The need however is greater than ever before, which is surprising, given the ability of contacting help in real time. So our sincerest salute goes to all of our colleagues – especially the women – who give so much without being rewarded or even recognized.

ENTROPY

March 14 is International Pi day. No, not pie day, rather Pi day. The mathematical constant that is the ratio of a circle's circumference to its diameter,
approximated as 3.14159. Although it is believed that the Babylonians were
the first to have calculated it to be about 3.125, Archimedes (287-212 BC)
is considered to be the first to calculate it accurately. Thus March 14 or the
fourteenth day of the third month of the year (3.14) is celebrated as Pi day
by mathematicians.

It is one of the constants in the laws of the universe that control and
regulate our lives. Although some laws like entropy point to chaos as being
another constant, it can be argued that the chaotic changes in themselves
are orderly.

In medicine too, entropy is considered by some to be the cause of
genetic mutation and degradation of our life due to accumulation of bad
mutations in the human genome. But genetic mutation happens in all living
things. The one thing, however, that is overlooked is the fact that at that same
rate, good mutations occurs as well. These good mutations too are passed
on from generation to generation and maybe the reason why many of our
children are smarter than we are. It is true that we are mortal but that too
is a universal constant and all living things, in fact, are mortal – as is the
universe itself. But what is mortality? The second law of thermo dynamic
indicates, "Energy must be spent in order to create order!" And the first
law of thermo dynamic indicates, "Energy cannot be created or destroyed!"
Then the third law of thermo dynamic (entropy) indicates, "Energy must

degrade to perform work." So if life is a form of energy, the mortality of it could be considered a change in its form and not necessarily the end of it.

The fact that more of us are realizing, researching, experimenting and working with this knowledge in itself is a proof of the advancement of our genome in good ways. For example, our progression in computer science is contributing to the enrichment of our understanding of the many natural laws. That comprehension too will enrich the way we will practice medicine in the future. Maybe we should just slough off our comfortable layer of old beliefs and embrace the chaos of the new information coming our way. That however does not mean to destroy or disregard old knowledge, traditions or customs. Rather it means to build upon their foundation and establish a just and equal world for all. A healthy world encourages the good mutational changes in our genome and a weak, diseased, and contaminated one degrades those mutational changes. The real question here is, how to use the technology at our disposal to make positive changes and mold the entropic energy to perform constructive work. It is said; "The HOWs in life are easy, the WHYs are the tough ones." But today we can say that; "We know what needs to be done, HOW to do them are the tough ones."

THE INFINITY OF A CONSTANT

As stated previously, March 14 is International Pi Day. The mathematical constant that is the ratio of a circle's circumference to its diameter is approximated as 3.1415926535….. The decimal number goes on forever. Contained within its string of decimals is every number pertaining to man's life, history, nature and cosmos. And if the decimals are converted into letters, you will find every word that ever existed, spoken and written. All the infinite possibilities of words rest within this one simple circle.

In our bodies too, the ratio of our consciousness or psyche to our physical being could be said to have infinite possibilities. Our body goes where the mind tells it to. Our mind works by the demands of our soul/ consciousness/ intellect/ psyche – or whatever we want to call it. Our actions are dictated by our desires, wishes and wants which in turn are based on our intelligence, education, experience, and wisdom. The more of these combinations we use, the better will be the outcome of our deeds. The possibilities of our actions are infinite. The choices we make may depend on the advice of others, on our teaching, or on a variety of outside influences. But the end result is *where we end up in our lives and what we have to live with.* Limited knowledge leads to limited and fewer choices and actions, wiser decisions produce healthier and happier outcomes.

Healthcare gives us many opportunities to find answers to our medical and mental problems. Wise and intelligent approaches lead to better outcomes. There are many options to the constant of man's need and our technology adds to those options. Indeed it is a wonderful time of history we live in and if prudent decisions are made, a bright future will surely be ours.

A SALUTE TO OUR NURSES

The rays of the sun coming through the open window of the hut woke me. Looking around the unfamiliar surroundings, I rose on an elbow and smelled the coffee.

"Good morning," she said smiling.

I sat on the cot and smiled back, "what time is it, did I oversleep?"

"Oh no. It is five thirty, you are fine."

She looked clean, fresh, happy and full of energy even in that early hour of the day. I wondered when she awoke or if she slept at all. She kept her composure throughout the time we were there.

It was the first day of our four-day visit to this remote mountain top community. I was there with three other providers – two dentists and an ophthalmologist. I was to provide general primary care. The village was far from any medical establishment – a two-day journey by horse and mule. The so-called clinic we were to work out of was a two-room hut ran by two nuns, one was an RN. We flew in on a small aircraft and landed on an open field cleared by the natives. A follow up visit for our eye doctor and one of the dentists. A first for me and the other dentist. We saw over two hundred patients in those four days and could have seen hundreds more. Their appreciation and gratitude toward us was contagious, even by the ones we didn't get to see. I felt ashamed and guilty to leave after our short stay.

Our missionary nun/RN had been there for many years, providing spiritual as well as medical care to the many Indians living throughout the mountains and valleys. She knew everyone by name, his or her medical and social problems. Acted as interpreter, assistant, immunizer, phlebotomist, and above all else; nurse. In our absence, she would be a provider, midwife, and dentist as well till the next group of volunteers arrived – whenever that would be. I learned much about caring from her on that short visit.

I have had the opportunity to meet and work with many nurses like her in my years of medical work. I learned more from them than all the schooling I got otherwise. Perhaps the greatest and most important lesson has been how to be compassionate in the face of adversity, care for everyone even when they themselves stop caring. How to teach while learning and learn while teaching. As Maya Angelou once said; "People will forget what you said, people will forget what you did, but people will never forget how you made them feel."

Today our world is in dire shortage of trained and dedicated nurses. Every country needs more of them – some more than others. Even here in our great rich country there is need for many more nurses. Philanthropists spend money on programs to provide healthcare to needy regions of the world but little on training nurses to deliver that care.

In this digital age, we can do much more in helping our nurses deliver their wonderful care to everyone around the world. Whether in a hut on a mountaintop, in a tent on the battlefield, on the streets of a famine driven city far away, or a state of the art hospital in an American or European city, they need our support and appreciation. We salute our dedicated and caring nurses everywhere.

READ ACROSS AMERICA

"I heirt my nee." Was the reason for his visit to our office, the young man wrote on his medical questionnaire when he signed in. He was a senior from a top high school in our town. He had driven himself to our office in a new BMW – indicating that he was from a well to do family. I found him well dressed and exceptionally polite. But then it was that spelling.

March 2nd is Read Across America day. A day established in honor of Dr. Seuss to motivate people to celebrate reading. It is a wonderful idea twenty years old. It is interesting to see it celebrated in this age of smart phones, computer tablets and electronic devices.

In our house, we didn't have a TV till my youngest was in high school. I was scorned about it by friends and neighbors alike. Some of my children would sneak over to the neighbor on Saturday mornings to watch cartoons. I was OK with it and pretended not to notice. We had the biggest library in the neighborhood, and so they became avid readers. My wife and I read to them every night and they looked forward to it even in their teenage years. Thank God, today they are all educated and successful in their lives.

Among the many books we read was, of course those by Dr. Seuss. My favorite of his – one that I feel should be mandatory reading for all college students – is *Did I ever tell you how lucky you are?*

Just like the little boy in the story listening to the happy old man living in the Desert of Drize, many of us feel blessed for all that we do have, rather than not. Health as well as wealth, education, freedom and security contribute to our overall happiness. Yet we take much for granted and that may make us malcontent and depressed, leading us to act irrationally and at times violently. Unfortunately our history is full of such incidents and it's getting worse. Recent school and mass shootings are examples of such tragedies. Many feel that social media is a great contributor to this problem. Maybe so, but it also could be the unbalanced available information that is leading to the wrong choices our people make. Much could be said about that here, but as our job is healthcare, we can start by practicing good and sound medicine. By implementing best practices into our work, we reduce much of the stress and anxiety in our own lives and that of our patients. Then maybe we can find time to read to our children and help them become balanced and intelligent adults. For as the purpose of *Read Across America* indicates; "Motivating children to read is an important factor in student achievement and creating lifelong successful readers. Research has shown that children who are motivated and spend more time reading do better in school." And in life!

APRIL

Of Note in April

April 4, 1802 (1887) – American social reformer Dorothea Dix was born in Hampden, Maine. While in her teens, she founded a home for girls in Boston. Later crusaded for humane conditions in prisons and insane asylums. During the American Civil War, she was superintendent of women nurses.

April 6, 1896 – After 1500 years, the Olympics was restarted in Athens, Greece.

April 8, 563 B.C. (483 B.C.) – Birthday of Buddha is celebrated by an estimated 350 million people worldwide.

April 10, 1847 (1911) – Joseph Pulitzer was born in Budapest, Hungary. He immigrated to America in 1864. After the Civil War he began working as a journalist and then as a publisher. He endowed the journalism school at Columbia University and established a fund for the Pulitzer Prizes, awarded annually for excellence in journalism.

April 13, 1919 – Acting British Brigadier-General Reginald Dyer ordered his troops to fire into a crowd of unarmed Indian civilians in Jallianwala Bagh, Amritsar, Punjab, killing at least 400 people and injuring a 1,000 more. It came to be known as The Jallianwala Bagh massacre.

April 15, 1817 – The first American school for the deaf was founded by Thomas H. Gallaudet and Laurent Clerc in Hartford, Connecticut.

April 19, 1995 – The domestic terrorist truck bombing of the Alfred P. Murrah Federal Building in Oklahoma City, Oklahoma, by Timothy McVeigh and Terry Nichols killed 168 and injured about 700 people.

April 25, 1967 – Colorado Governor John Love, signed the first law legalizing abortion in cases which a panel of three doctors unanimously agreed.

DIABETES IN THE CARIBBEAN

Dominica, like many other islands in the Caribbean Sea is a volcanic out-cropping located between two French islands, Guadeloupe to the north and Martinique to the south. The extreme mountainous terrain makes it nearly impossible to build an adequate airport to receive large aircraft. So the only way there is by boat or a small plane – though that is changing. The island is literally a nature paradise with hundreds of waterfalls and lush jungle full of exotic fauna, birds and reptiles – none poisonous or dangerous. It is home to the only and last Carib Indian Tribe. They live on a small reservation on the east side of the island. The majority of the population is of African descent, remnants of freed slaves. In the past, the island was managed by the French, then English until their independence in 1978. Healthcare is provided by a handful of doctors and providers from other countries. Several members of the island's elite have gone to medical schools in Europe, US and Canada and manage the only hospital there.

Hurricane David demolished the island in the late 70s. I, with many others, volunteered to help rebuild. I spent about three months on the island caring for the sick and injured. Despite the utter devastation of the place, surprisingly not many were injured. The people, being used to the Caribbean storms, took shelter in the hills and out of the way of the destructive forces of the hurricane. The poor economy kept many goods unavailable, still I found the people very healthy. Apparently lack of adequate roads necessitated them to walk everywhere. Crossing the many rivers of the island kept them clean and the jungle supplied them with many wild fruits such as mangoes. Limited interaction with outsiders kept communicable diseases away. Except for some cases of STD, the population was healthy. I have mentioned many stories from my short stay there as appropriate in different parts of this book. Much of what I noticed there applies to other islands as well, although the rate of modernization has made the advances of healthcare or lack of it more rapid or slow.

Since my visit however, the island has been discovered and the introduction of western diet and food has brought with it maladies such as diabetes, high blood pressure, and heart problems. From under-nutrition to over-eating has lead to an upsurge in chronic non-communicable diseases. A price for advancement, the island did not have to pay. Today the increased number of diabetic amputations among young people on many of these islands is causing alarm and major concern.

Despite of all the challenges our world is dealing with today, our technology is making advances on many fronts – healthcare included. If our social issues could be curbed, faster progress could be made in these areas. It took Dr. Jonas Salk, two and half years to develop the polio vaccine in 1955. Today we developed the Covid-19 vaccine in less than 10 months. In many Sci-Fi TV series like *Star Trek*, medical officers develop vaccines for alien pathogens in matter of days, even hours. We can only hope one day our science is as efficient. We have the wherewithal to eradicate maladies such as diabetes, cancer, heart disease and others. Mankind is on track and moving forward. We just need to ensure to advance the entire humanity and not just a chosen few. Then places like Dominica and other Caribbean and far away islands will remain a nature paradise not only for visitors but the local residents as well.

TELEHEALTH and LEPROSY, BBS and STROKE

Since the invention of Internet, people in all walks of life have been trying to apply it to their business or cause. Medicine is no exception and indeed it has received much attention in the many ways its use can benefit the population of the world.

Many organizations are working on making the use of this tool seamless and beneficial without undo regulatory hindrance. Groups like the Federation of State Medical Boards (FSMB), American Telemedicine Association (ATA), American Nurses Association, UNM Project ECHO and many others are working on these efforts.

In reading through forums on the ATA and other websites, one question keeps coming up. How should an organization or hospital handle telehealth privileges for its providers? It seems that suddenly, organizations feel the need to regulate this age-old practice. But if we step back and look at the way we have been practicing medicine forever, we see that providers have always used telecommunication and consulted with their patients and one another regarding their care. Even primitive medicine-men consulted one another by smoke signals or drumbeats:

"Child sick, feel hot. What to do?"

I would argue that, this too is telehealth! We are just carrying this concept into the 21st century technology and exchanging drums for Internet. So the idea that we need new regulations to do this is ludicrous.

It is not healthcare providers who are asking for regulations. It is our legal colleagues and their bean counter friends who see financial gain in this, that are asking for it. But once we start down this road, we will regulate ourselves out of business.

Here is Dr. Peter Yellowlees, the 2017 President of ATA's response to this;

> *I am concerned about this discussion and do not believe that telemedicine should be privileged in any special way as part of a credentialing process. I have been practicing tele-med for many years and have never heard of this occurring previously. All that is happening is raising yet another administrative barrier to tele-medicine, which is the last thing we want.*

The Federation of State Medical Boards' work on the Interstate Medical Licensure Compact directly affects the very practice of telemedicine. Without clear and undemanding national licensing, all efforts toward the real practice of telehealth will be difficult. The entire philosophy of Telehealth and Telemedicine is the ability to bring needed help to underserved and rural communities of our country without undue regulatory hindrance. Many of these areas are across state lines, making the need for the 'Compact' essential.

Another urgent call for telehealth is the need for specialty medicine in many parts of the globe. According to the Orpha and Global Genes websites, there are approximately 7,000 rare diseases and disorders affecting more than 300 million people worldwide with only a few centers specializing in their treatment. The Compact would help the specialists in these centers care for patients everywhere.

It is imperative to realize that the importance of Telehealth, Telemedicine, and Tele-education is attracting the attention of tens of thousands of practitioners, regulators and legislatures. Our small world is getting ever more populated and despite the fact that we elect representatives to address the many shortfalls it faces, the challenges seem to mount rather than be solved. No place is this issue in more dire need of immediate attention than in healthcare. The future of our troubled world depends on what we can resolve today. Here is an example of the importance of this critical issue: In 2016, India reported that their health department has checked 320 million people for leprosy – still an international problem.

The medical school I attended was affiliated with the US Public Health Hospital on Staten Island, NY. It was the early 1970s and the Vietnam War was still on. Due to the need for healthcare providers in the military, there was a shortage of medical personnel in the private sector. This was particularly acute in such places as public health hospitals and clinics like ours. As a result, many foreign doctors were employed to fill the need. This brought with it numerous challenges but just as many opportunities as well. Several of these doctors, for example, were from Latin America and the Far East; like China, Korea or the Philippines. Besides their Western education, many had Eastern medical experiences which came in handy at the time.

Our hospital was the only one on the East Coast that treated Hansen's Disease (Leprosy). Several of our East Asian and South American providers had good experiences in the treatment of this disease from their home countries and thus were put in charge of that clinic. With the advances in the treatment of this disease, the number of cases was small. Many of our patients were from the Caribbean, Central and South America. They stayed with relatives in the NY area and were treated by us. Often, the biggest challenge in treating these patients was not their health problem, but rather the economical and financial hardship their care in NY created. They needed follow up every few months, which made it necessary to stay in NY till their treatment was completed. They were usually from indigent families and going back and forth to their home countries was not a realistic option. Some did go back and we usually never saw them again.

Today, with the advent of telehealth and telemedicine, we can treat many of them in their own countries and at home. But only if we can overcome the many political and bureaucratic obstacles.

In a recent telehealth meeting, Doctor Bob Haws, a Pediatrics-Nephrologist from Marshfield Clinic told us about his work with Bardet-Biedl Syndrome (BBS). He told us that; "There are only 2500 patients in the United States that have this disease and Marshfield Clinic is the specializing center in the treatment of it. Since these patients live all over the United States and the world, it makes it more challenging to provide care for them. To expect these people to travel to Wisconsin for treatment and follow-up is a hardship and usually unaffordable. Most could be treated in their hometown via telehealth, but state regulatory agencies wont allow it, as they require Marshfield clinicians be licensed in their state. This is unreasonable for there are maybe only one or two patients in that state with such an illness. To have specialists hold licensure in every state to treat a few patients with rare diseases in that state is costly and unattainable. Thus the burden falls on patients to travel to specialists' hometowns for treatment. If they could use telehealth in their work, the burden, cost and hardship on the patients and the providers would be reduced dramatically. Yet unreasonable licensing requirements make such logical means of care unavailable."

Here is another example of how Telehealth can help our health-care system;

In a monthly meeting, back in April 2017; Dr. Howard Yonus, along with Dr. Collin Semper from University of New Mexico (UNM) dept of Neurosurgery reported on a federal award they received to use telemedicine in caring for stroke patients. The enormous difference it made to get care to patients in rural areas quickly and the great savings to all involved by keeping the patients in their hometown and local care facilities. Historically stroke patients were routinely transferred to major medical centers such as UNM. The enormous cost and wasted time in transport – whether by ambulance or aircraft – has been non-productive and often at the patients peril.

The use of telemedicine to treat stroke patients has been a Godsend. The UNM experience reveals that it has saved 20 million dollars in airfare transfers alone and added 12 million dollars to the bottom line of rural hospitals. Converting 80% of transfers to 80% that were kept at home.

They reported that telemedicine provides 24/7 consult and second consult within 24 hours. It avoids late transfers as well by helping hospitalists and local providers decide and care for patients locally (this was reported by UNM in the *Journal of Medical Economics* Volume 21, 2018 - Issue 4).

It is noteworthy that neurosurgical telemedicine consultations have lowered transfers to 15%. Of those retained at local hospitals, none transferred later, causing substantial savings to CMS and other payers. The small percentages that were transferred often needed surgery. It is also significant that under the leadership of Dr. Paul Roth, Chancellor of UNM Health Science Center and Dean of the UNM Medical School, and Dr. Margaret McGrew of the UNM's School of Family Medicine, the university has been in the forefront of this transformation. It is also worth mentioning that UNM's School of Family Practice has consistently been on US News and World Report's top 10 colleges' annual listing.

There are many other diseases and cases like BBS, Hansen's Disease, and stroke that could effectively be treated through new communication tools, if we could set aside our prejudices and unreasonable need for turf control. Advances can be made on many of these rare diseases and universal healthcare become a true reality.

MAYA ANGELOU AT AAOS

April 4, 1928, was the birthday of poet Maya Angelou.

In 1999, she was the Presidential Guest Speaker at the American Academy of Othopaedic Surgeons' annual meeting in Anaheim, California. In his introduction of Maya Angelou, Dr. James D. Heckman, President of the Academy, said he chose Angelou as speaker to put a humanistic spirit into medical education. "We are overwhelmed with new science and new technology," he said. "It has been said that we are fine technicians, but lack the sensitivity and caring touch so often desired by our patients. With those thoughts in mind I have selected Maya Angelou, who I know will bring some balance and much beauty to these proceedings."

I was an attendee at that conference and was pleasantly impressed by her speech. I was particularly tickled when she started singing on how the "Toe bone connected to the foot bone, foot bone connected to the ankle bone, ankle bone connected to the shin bone,…" on and on to the skull bone - to thousands of orthopaedic surgeons.

After her speech, I met her and upon learning my name, she began speaking Arabic to me. She was disappointed that my knowledge of that language was very limited. I recall her quoting an African divine saying, encouraging the orthopaedic surgeons to inspire others by "becoming a rainbow in their clouds." She told us the story of her son who was paralyzed in an auto accident but recovered and was able to walk under the care of an orthopaedic surgeon. She gratefully told the audience; "It's amazing what you are able to do, and how many lives you touch. Even at the worst time, one can see a possibility of hope."

Recalling her childhood in segregated Arkansas, she said, "Stamps, Arkansas, with its dust and hate and narrowness was as South as it was possible to get. One needs to know that others have had sad times. One survives with compassion, humor and style."

Later in her life, she lived in Egypt and Ghana, working as a journalist. She was over forty years old when, on the advise of a novelist friend; James Baldwin, began to write. Her first autobiography; *I Know Why the Caged Bird Sings (1969)* was a great success. She went on to write many more books including *Oh Pray My Wings Are Gonna Fit Me Well (1975)*. She died on May 28, 2014 in Winston-Salem, NC. She was eighty-six years old.

"Since life is our most precious gift, let us dedicate all our conscious lives to liberation of the human mind and spirit," she told her avid audience. "We human beings are more alike than unalike. Everybody wants healthy children, safe streets and love. Everybody wants someplace to party on Saturday night."

In less than twenty years from that speech, new communication tools have completely changed the way we correspond, interact and learn from each other. Today we are overwhelmed with new science and technology but these tools also reveal the existence of many Angelous in our world. Many of them in our own world of medicine and education. By embracing their teachings and learning of the adversities they had to overcome to be the teachers they are, we too can be liberators of human mind and spirit and serve those who need us, not for monetary gains, but for the pure joy of helping our fellow human beings. As Angelou said; *When you learn, teach. When you get, give.*

INSTINCTS

The scorpion appeared from under the sack of beans and headed across the busy bazaar toward me. I was surprised that it escaped the many feet crossing the narrow passageway. I sheepishly smiled to myself and said; *"Your luck will run out when you get to me"* and slowly raised my foot to squish it. The old man sitting next to me placed his walking stick gently but firmly on my foot and pressed it back to the ground. I turned to him surprised; "The scorpion is the warden of the desert. You should not disturb it." He said with a stern, yet warm and gentle tone.

I was about eight or nine in the bazaar with my grandmother shopping. When she went into one of the stalls, I sat on the stone bench outside the store next to the old man. His warm and fatherly voice calmed my questioning look.

"What if it stings someone?" I asked.

"It will not, unless it is threatened or disturbed. It is its nature to sting in self-defense. To hurt a creature who acts out of instinct is a sin. "

Respect for the environment and the world around us is not something you learn from books. It is something that has to be woven into the fabric of life as we grow. My Grandmother used to carefully brush the crumbs off her dinner plate and place it into the garden, saying; *"It may be just a bread crumb to us but it is a full meal to an ant."* Such reverence for all living things is vanishing from our cultures. Some feel that today's world of high rises is isolating us from our environment. Making us forget that hundreds of feet below our apartments, there is still a living planet supporting our very existence. We no longer value instincts, nature, or the needs of others. But instincts are in every living thing, including us humans. Society, religion, and cultural ethics further demand certain actions from us. Sadly, today's world cares less and less for such values and has forced millions of people into circumstances beyond their control. And when they follow their instincts and teachings to protect themselves and their families, they are criticized or worse. Our information technology should make us more aware and caring of our environment not less. But unfortunately that does not seem to be the case.

Healthcare, too, is a necessity many seek when they are ill or injured. To deny them that help and allow them to suffer is inhumane, no matter on which side of the fence they may be. And maybe if they receive the help they need, they will not cross borders or climb fences. It takes so little to care.

Practicing from the Heart

TWO

THE SACRED HUMAN BODY

"I like it when you help me, Reza" Al Rosen used to say. "You don't talk a lot and you don't suck a lot."

Al Rosen was a legendary doctor and an avid skier in Taos, New Mexico. An all around country doctor and surgeon, he practiced the old way. He made house calls, held patient's hands when he talked to them and knew everyone by their first name. He first came to Taos in the late 1930s. Over the years, along with Doctors Pond and DeVeaux, they became the corner stone of medicine in Taos and Northern New Mexico. Although Al Rosen was not a board certified surgeon of any kind, he did most of the surgical cases and obstetrics in Taos in those days. Before I arrived in Northern New Mexico in the early 1970s, no other PA had assisted him. Many young residents from UNM School of Medicine rotated through Taos and often helped Dr. Rosen in surgery. But he felt that most of the younger doctors who assisted him wanted to *constantly do something*, thus they ended up hindering rather than helping him. "They pull the wound toward themselves so that *they* can see better." Al used to say. "And in the zeal of being active in the case, constantly use the suction tube even when there is nothing to suck and block my view. I have to almost fight them to do the surgery."

I met Dr. Rosen soon after arriving in the area and when he learned of my surgical and orthopaedic background, he asked me to assist him. My knowledge of traction setup also helped keep more patients from being transferred away from home. Shortly after however, Steve Halmstad PA joined his practice and became his primary surgical assistant. But because of my orthopaedic surgical experience, I continued to help him on many such cases that were not referred out.

Al's surgical room was always quiet. He did not like anyone to play the radio or music or talk loud in his operating suite. "The auditory nerve is not anesthetized!" he used to say. "Unnecessary noises can cause subconscious anxiety and the patient will dislike the surgical experience. By keeping quiet and paying attention to our work the surgery will have a more positive and rewarding outcome."

On the ski slopes of Taos Mountain however, Al was a daredevil. Flying down black diamond runs and around hairpin turns made him a different kind of a legend. Hard to believe that such a mild mannered doctor was such a risk taker. He was enough of a regular presence on the ski slopes that they named one of the black diamond runs after him. *Al's Run* challenges many expert skiers even today. In his later years, he was often seen skiing down the slopes wearing an oxygen tank and mask. Al Rosen died in October of 1982 but his legacy lives on. I learned a lot from Al Rosen and others like him.

When I first entered the operating room at the ripe age of fourteen, I was shaking with excitement and fear. Excitement for entering such a sacred realm and fear of screwing something up. As I have indicated earlier, I was given the job by a doctor friend of my father. He became my benefactor and his devotion to his work, strong regard for his patients and love of teaching was the greatest gift I received during the early days of my medical career. He often told me, "it is harder to assist than to do the surgery because the assistant must think twice. First he must realize what the surgeon is doing and then act accordingly to help him accomplish it."

"Don't watch me," he would start, "watch my hand, watch where I put the instrument, the needle, the suture. What is the purpose of my action and what can *you* do to improve it's outcome."

So it was that I got introduced to his assistant; Ibrahïm. He was a burley, kind looking middle aged and stoutly religious gentleman who had been working with my benefactor ever since he opened his private hospital. Ibrahïm was, for all practical purposes, illiterate. He read very poorly and could not write to save his life. But he knew and could identify every part of the intestine and abdominal tissue and fissure. Over the years he had intently watched his operating surgeon's every move and had seen his share of successes and failures. Watching the two of them was a treat, as though only one brain moved those four hands in concert. Ibrahïm started every procedure with a prayer – quietly, under his breath, he would pray for the safety of the patient and his/her rapid recovery. Not once did I hear him pray for himself, or the surgeon. Always for the patient so that he or she could return to the family waiting for them, healed and recovered. What I learned from him helped me cope with many challenges of ever day medicine through the rest of my career. "The human body is sacred" he used to say. "The very breath of God has given it life, treat it with reverence and respect and it will repay you by healing well."

Years later and halfway around the world, I had an opportunity to be involved in an FDA clinical trial of a cementless, porous coated press-fit stem hip implant for a major orthopaedic device maker. I moved to Lubbock, Texas in the late 80s to assist with the process by helping a recruited orthopaedic surgeon there. While living and working there, I got to work with several orthopaedic surgeons. I came to know and highly respect another ortho-paedic physician who was from India named Gurdev Gill. He used very few instruments to do his surgeries and was of the philosophy that instruments injured the tissue and one should be cognizant of their use – a strange thing to hear from an orthopaedic surgeon who cut bone and tissue and replaced them with metal and plastic. Yet there it was. His patients recovered faster and better than many other surgeons I worked with.

In that job, I was also trained and acted as a salesman for that com-pany, thus got a good understanding of the mentality of the world of medical device sales and business.

One reward of assisting many doctors is that you appreciate the dif-ference between good surgeons and the others. This can teach you a lot in medicine. The process of assisting many surgeons with different ideology and techniques could make the job of a PA assistant difficult. But different approaches to a problem is a powerful learning tool. The PA's knowledge of the different approaches becomes very helpful when problems arise and can make the PA a valuable member of the surgical team.

In all my years of teaching, I have had many student precepts. I try to impart this knowledge that was taught to me over the years. To my students I say; *when you assist, assist fully and be cognizant of the patient's well-being. Be gentle to the tissue you are working on, especially if the doctor you are assisting is rough in his work. Be kind to the tissue and the tissue will be kind to you and heal well* is what I learned from the likes of Doctors; Gill, Rosen, assistant Ibrahïm, Grand-Lady and others. Over the years I have heard back from many of my thankful students who claimed that their mindful approach has made them a better assistant on surgical cases.

MAY

Of Note in May

May 1st – May Day, a spring festival and a Labor Day observed in socialist countries.

May 5, 1818 (1883) – Karl Marx was born in Treves, Germany.

May 5, 1961 – Alan Shepard became the first American in space.

May 6, 1856 (1939) – Psychoanalyst Sigmund Freud was born in Freiberg, Moravia.

May 7, 1992 – The 27th Amendment to the U.S. Constitution was ratified, prohibiting Congress from giving itself pay raises.

May 8, 1828 (1910) – International Red Cross founder and Nobel Prize winner Henri Dunant was born in Geneva, Switzerland.

May 10, 1994 – Nelson Mandela was inaugurated as president of South Africa.

May 11, 1969 – The Battle of "Hamburger Hill" began in Viet Nam. Over a 10-day period, U.S. troops repeatedly engaged in desperate hand-to-hand combat with the North Vietnamese. After finally securing the hill, American military staff decided to abandon the position, which the North Vietnamese retook shortly thereafter. The battle highlighted the senselessness of the war.

May 12, 1820 (1910) – Florence Nightingale was born in Florence, Italy.

May 14, 1686 (1736) – German physicist Gabriel Fahrenheit was born in Danzig, Germany. He introduced the use of mercury in thermometers and greatly improved their accuracy.

May 14, 1796 – Smallpox vaccine was developed by Dr. Edward Jenner.

May 14, 1942 – An Act of Congress allowed women to enlist for non-combat duties in the Women's Auxiliary Army Corps (WAAC).

May 17, 1954 – In Brown v. Board of Education, the U.S. Supreme Court unanimously ruled that segregation of public schools "solely on the basis of race" denies black children "equal educational opportunity". Thurgood Marshall had argued the case before the Court. He went to become the first African-American appointed to the Supreme Court by President Johnson in 1967.

May 18, 1980 – Mount St. Helens volcano erupted in southwestern Washington State. The first major eruption since 1857.

May 21, 1881 – Clara Barton founded The American Red Cross.

May 23, 1646 (1911) – The first American female attorney Arabella Mansfield was born near Burlington, Iowa (as Belle Aurelia Babb). She was instrumental in the founding of the Iowa Suffrage Society in 1870.

May 24, 1844 – Telegraph inventor Samuel Morse sent the first official telegraph message, "What hath God wrought?" from the Capitol building in Washington, D.C., to Baltimore.

May 25, 1803 (1882) – Ralph Waldo Emerson was born in Boston, Massachusetts.

May 28, 1961 – Amnesty International was founded by London lawyer Peter Berenson.

May 31, 1819 (1892) – American poet Walt Whitman was born in Long Island, NY.

May 31, 1921 – Mobs of armed white people attacked and killed 300 black residents of Greenwood District of Tulsa, Oklahoma, and burned their neighborhood.

THE VALUE OF LISTENING

Cheikh Ibrahima Niang, a professor of medical and social anthropology at the Cheikh Anta Diop University in Dakar, Senegal, was asked by the World Health Organization (WHO) in July 2014, to investigate community attitudes to Ebola virus disease. His report was published by WHO on February 2015 (its worthwhile to look this up: *Ebola Diaries: Lessons In Listening*).

The most important thing he learned was that too many people from other countries went to these disease stricken areas and told the people there what to do. But no one was listening to what the locals had to say. Dr. Niang's first assessment was that before you can create effective messages, you have to listen first. People needed to be heard and given the knowledge that gives them the power to make their own decisions.

"So we did a lot of listening, without making any noise." He said, "Our approach was humble, humane, discreet and focused on their concerns. No official cars, no flag waving, no uniforms. We did not make a show. In fact, WHO was the only organization that sat with villagers and listened to them for hours. And they were anxious to speak with us. Angry, frustrated, scared of this disease that was killing them and of the many recommendations that clashed with their belief systems, they felt misunderstood and abandoned by the whole world. It became clear that resistance was a way people affirmed their position when their dignity felt threatened. Once heard and understood, communities felt reassured, violence diminished and as they felt that their dignity and trust was restored, we were well received."

It is no different here in our country. As the demography of our world changes, rural communities become more isolated and alienated. Often even forgotten. Then when disaster strikes, all kinds of people converge on them with all kinds of ideas and recommendations. Too many messages have a way of being misunderstood and ignored. A good example of this was the chaos people experienced during Hurricane Katrina. Many agencies and organizations were conveying conflicting information. The end result was that thousands of people were left without any help.

If there has been one thing that I have learned in all my years of working in healthcare, it is the value of listening. Patients often tell us what is wrong with them, and in more times than not – even how to treat them. All we have to do then is confirm their suspicions and make an objective diagnosis, start or continue their treatment and charge them an office visit. Nothing will make a practitioner more likeable than good communication and in contrast bad communication will cost us. In the many years I served on the NM Medical Board, I noticed that the number one complaint against practitioners was lack of proper communication. Almost in every instance, the practitioner did everything correctly and the patient was treated properly. But the procedure was not communicated well and the patient left confused and dissatisfied. So I tell all my students; "Make your patients like you! People who like you won't sue you!"

As I previously said, the good Lord has given us one mouth, but two ears. If we listen twice as much as we talk to our patients, we will be a great practitioner and have no problems. Listening makes good communication possible, even for lousy communicators.

Today we have the gift of new communication tools. Proper use of these technologies can keep the people everywhere informed, educated and prepared for future calamities, epidemics and disasters. To use the old proverb; *an ounce of prevention is worth a pound of cure.* Proper communication can do that effectively, cheaply and timely.

STORIES WE HEARD AT MEETINGS

Stories always add a level of understanding, expectation and intrigue to a conversation or presentation. They also substantiate the presenter's point of view or dire need for help. At the many meetings of the American Telemedicine Association (ATA), we heard stories of cases that were helped by telehealth in situations large and small. In the ATA meeting in Minneapolis in 2016 for example, a woman, who was helped by telemedicine for her mental condition, presented at one of the plenary sessions. At another session, Dr. David Shulkin, Under Secretary for Veterans Administration reported the many ways telemedicine was used to treat veterans in the system. Dr. John Noseworthy, President and CEO of Mayo Clinic told of how Mayo uses telemedicine. David B. Hoyt, Executive Director of American College of Surgeons, and Jack Resneck, of American Medical Association and many others all had their own stories.

Likewise many stories told at meetings of Project ECHO – perhaps the most successful telehealth and tele-education program around – show not only how these programs work, but how the humanity of them is what brings the needed help to the masses.

But the stories that mattered the most, intriguing, heart warming, or even depressing were those heard at dinner tables or chance encounters. On the way to or from the different sessions or just waiting in line for a cup of coffee. Like the medical student from Nigeria who is perplexed about the dire and immense needs of his country at the meeting seeking guidance on how to deal with such insurmountable need while fighting the bureaucracy of his native land. A Colombian doctor who wants to bring care to the indigent people who are losing their habitat deep in the jungles and are unaware of Internet, phones and even electricity. And the Canadian doctor who was so proud of turning the dire healthcare situation in his isolated small town into a rousing success through telehealth. And still yet the Syrian doctor who is trying desperately to help the innocent people of his war torn hometown. They were all stories shared, overheard and discussed, revealing the tenderness of the human soul, and the humanity of our species to care for others.

One noteworthy point that becomes very clear and emphasizes the call for our efforts is the universality of the need. From little isolated islands in the South Pacific with a small population to large countries in African deserts and South American jungles with millions, the need is there and it is dire. As the economies of the world get stretched and environmental challenges increase, the healthcare needs increase, especially for the poor and isolated people around the world.

In addressing the Senate Committee on Commerce, Science, and Transportation awhile back, astrophysicist and space exploration advocate Neil deGrasse Tyson said, "Any nation at any time has the capacity to create a hero, just has to have ambition with goals set so that one among us steps forward and accepts those risks." Today many heroes are waiting to be provided goals and opportunities to step forward, accept risks and move their nation, society, and the world forward. Many of them are healthcare providers anxious to be the hero in their field. We owe it to them to create the needed roads. Telehealth and tele-education are such avenues; let us embrace their mission and vision. Let's encourage and assist our fellow colleagues to expand the vision to all corners of our small planet. Let's help them be the heroes.

MENTAL HEALTH
AWARENESS MONTH

Much has been written about the origin, reason, diagnosis, and treatment of mental illness. From the time of Hippocrates, who first declared that mental illness has a physical and medical foundation and not a religious or evil basis to Freud with his theory that mental disorders such as schizophrenia resulted from unconscious conflicts originating in early childhood, to today when mental disorders are primarily seen as a biological disorder of the brain. Yet critics still call for a radical rethinking of mental disorders, not as disease processes with many diagnostic labels, but as subjective and meaningful experiences of both personal and socio-cultural reasons. Though no one can deny that psychological and social stressors play important roles in triggering episodes of illness, we have to keep in mind that definitions of mental health are at best subjective. All in all, they reveal the intricacy and complexity of the problem.

Add to this, the changes our modern life has made to the family and social structures and one can appreciate the challenges of dealing with this dilemma. The complication of these stresses touches all levels of our society. Even our own profession is not immune as about 400 doctors commit suicide every year. Furthermore when our politicians downplay the importance of the problem and decide that the government is not responsible for the problem so it should not be liable for it. This adds even more to the quagmire of dealing with it. The acuteness of this problem peaked in the 1980s when a large number of mental health hospitals and care centers were closed and their patients discharged into the streets. Many became homeless and out of necessity resorted to a life of petty crime just to survive and thus ended up in our prison system - costing the taxpayers more than it would have cost to care for them in the mental health facilities.

Sometimes even just a mental health crisis center or safe house could be all a person in distress needs to rest and heal. A few years back, a friend of ours came home one day to find her teenage son murdered by an intruder. Even though she was a psychiatric nurse herself, she was having a great deal of difficulty dealing with it even weeks after the event. Understandably, the overwhelming circumstance demanded that she get away from those sur-roundings. My wife and I offered her to come and stay with us for a while. We lived in the country and she readily accepted our offer. Although no one can truly forget such calamity, the interlude gave her healing time.

To deal with these problems and dilemma, experts like Rachel Pruchno Ph.D. suggest that we should bring back the mental asylums. But the very negative connotations attached to the concept of an asylum turns everyone off. Yet the problem is not the place for mentally ill people rather the negative stigma attached to it. The enormity of the problem shows the need for more resources to treat people with mental illness. The need for more psychiatrists, psychologists, and social workers. More inpatient facilities and integrated outpatient therapies so that people with mental illness are not homeless or imprisoned. We need to overhaul these infrastructures, not to eliminate them.

In this restructuring, telecommunication can play an enormous role. The majority of these people can be treated effectively with simple supervi-sion by a professional. By involving family members, many could be managed at home. With a little direction, family practitioners could care for a good percentage of them in their office. And the more serious cases could be cared for in institutions run primarily by well-trained midlevel and auxiliary healthcare providers. Technology could be the solution to a major part of mental health treatment, its usage can be enhanced and communication between parties improved. The means and facilities for this technology are available. We now need to use it, revolutionize it, grow it, and popularize it for the benefit of everyone.

MEMORIAL DAY

Memorial Day is in May, when we remember all those who gave their lives to defend our country. It's noteworthy that a year after the end of the Civil War, in April 1866, four women of Columbus, Mississippi gathered together to decorate the graves of the Confederate soldiers buried in their town. They also felt moved to honor the Union soldiers buried there and to note the grief of their families by decorating their graves as well. The story of their gesture of humanity and reconciliation is now told and retold in Mississippi as being the occasion of the original Memorial Day.

We should remember however that many in that war and since have lost their lives by receiving improper care in the hospitals after they were wounded. Medicine has always played a big role in military history. On May 19 in 1822, for example, the first naval medical school was opened at the Philadelphia Navy Yard to train physicians to care for the special needs of sailors and soldiers, yet we lost many of our wounded in the wars that followed.

Throughout history, as armies grew and weapons improved, the care of the sick and wounded became increasingly important. Cleanliness, for example, kept pestilence away in the Roman Army. The Roman soldiers bathed regularly even when on campaign. Cleanliness was recognized and reduced the incidence of wound infection. Acetum or vinegar was used extensively in wound cleaning by Roman physicians. A practice that continued for a long time but was lost during the Dark Ages.

Florence Nightingale and her trained nurses re-introduced basic standards of hygiene and sanitation thus lowering the mortality rate from 44 percent to 2 percent by the end of the Crimean War.

As an Air Force Medic, I did my share of caring for war wounded, ours as well as others. There is nothing like the emptiness in the eyes of an injured soldier who realizes that his/her life is changed forever. We owe it to them to give them our most undivided attention. Today's militaries are equipped with state of the art technology to attend to the sick and wounded on the battlefields and field hospitals. Yet back home our veterans lack proper care, especially in many rural communities.

Another heart-warming Memorial Day story is that of the Vietnam Veterans Peace and Brotherhood Chapel in the mountains north of Angle Fire, New Mexico (search the Internet for more information).

Following the death of their son, U.S. Marine Corps First Lieutenant Victor David Westphall III, Jeanne and Dr. Victor Westphall decided to build a memorial in his honor and the fifteen men that died with him near Con Thien, South Vietnam on May 22, 1968, and the Vietnam Veterans Peace and Brotherhood Chapel in Angle Fire, New Mexico was erected. The Chapel was dedicated on May 22, 1971, the 3rd anniversary of the death of their son. It was the first major memorial created to honor the veterans of the Vietnam War and inspired the establishment of the Vietnam Veterans Memorial in Washington D.C., which was completed ten years later in 1982.

I was working at a small clinic in the resort town of Red River, New Mexico in the late 70s and early 80s and as a Vietnam era veteran myself was happy to witness the beginning of it all. Circa 1982, a group of veterans and motorcycle enthusiasts made a pilgrimage to the site to honor their fallen comrades and to visit the one of a kind memorial. Since there are no amenities in the immediate vicinity of the Memorial, the bikers continued on to Red River - about 20 miles deeper in the mountains. Somehow the word got out in that era of no Internet and many more made the trip the next year and every year since, so that the 2018's Memorial Day event attracted about 20,000 to Red River and Angle Fire, New Mexico.

Although I no longer practice and have not done so in Red River for many years, the event brings back many memories. I am happy to report that the clinic I helped start in 1979 is still in operation there.

JUNE

Of note in June

June 2, 1740 (1814) – Marquis de Sade was born in Paris. His acts of extreme cruelty and violence resulted in the term *sadism* to describe gratification in inflicting pain.

June 3, 1993 – Sabrina Gonzalez Pasterski (The Physics Girl) was born. Considered by many to be the next Einstein.

June 7, 1965 – The U.S. Supreme Court struck down a Connecticut law banning contraception and guaranteed the right to privacy, including matters of birth control.

June 10, 1929 – Edward O. Wilson was born in Birmingham, Alabama. He is a proponent of sociobiology, the study of the genetic basis of social behavior of all animals, including humans.

June 11, 1880 (1973) – American politician Jeannette Rankin was born in Missoula, Montana. She was the first woman elected to the U.S. Congress.

June 13, 1966 – The U.S. Supreme Court ruled in the case of *Miranda v. Arizona* that an accused person must be apprised of certain rights before police questioning.

June 14, 1777 – John Adams introduced a resolution before Congress mandating a United States flag with thirteen stripes, alternating red and white, representing the thirteen states. And thirteen stars, white on a blue field, representing a new constellation. This anniversary is celebrated each year in the U.S. as Flag Day.

June 14, 1864 (1915) – Alois Alzheimer was born in Markbreit am Mainz, Germany. In 1907, he published an article first describing 'Alzheimer' a degenerative disease, affecting nerve cells of the brain and leading to severe memory impairment and progressive loss of mental faculties.

June 14, 1951 – Univac 1, the world's first commercial computer was unveiled in Philadelphia. It was installed at the Census Bureau.

June 15, 1215 – King John set his seal to Magna Carta, guaranteeing basic rights that have since become the foundation of modern democracies around the world.

June 16, 1920 (1980) – Author and photographer John Griffin was born in Dallas, Texas. He darkened his white skin posing as a black man traveling through the deep South. He wrote a journal and published it as; *Black Like Me*.

June 16, 1963 – Russian Valentina Tereshkova, 26, became the first woman in space.

June 18, 1983 – Dr. Sally Ride became the first American woman in space.

June 19, 1953 – Julius and Ethel Rosenberg were executed at Sing Sing Prison in New York. They had been found guilty of providing information on the atomic bomb to the Soviet Union during 1944-45.

June 19, 1903 (1941) – Baseball star Lou Gehrig was born in New York City. He contracted the degenerative muscle disease Amyotrophic Lateral Sclerosis (ALS), now called 'Lou Gehrig's disease,' and died of it on June 2, 1941.

June 21, 1905 (1980) – French philosopher Jean-Paul Sartre was born in Paris.

June 25, 1990 – The U.S. Supreme Court ruled (5-4) that it was unconstitutional for any state to require, without providing other options, a minor to notify both parents before obtaining an abortion.

June 25, 1991 – The republics of Croatia and Slovenia declared their independence from Yugoslavia resulting in ethnic rivalries between Serbians and Croatians. In 1992, a campaign of 'ethnic cleansing,' was started by the Serbs against the Muslims. At least two million people became refugees, and about 200,000 were missing and presumed dead.

June 26, 1945 – The United Nations Charter was signed in San Francisco by 50 nations. The Charter was ratified on October 24, 1945.

June 28, 1906 (1972) – Physicist Maria Goeppert Mayer was born in Kattowitz, Germany. She participated in the Manhattan Project – the building of the first atomic bomb. She later became the first American woman to win the Nobel Prize in 1963.

June 28, 1919 – The signing of the Treaty of Versailles formally ended World War I.

June 29, 1861 (1939) – William Mayo was born in LeSeuer, Minnesota. He was one of the Mayo brothers – pioneers of the concept of the group practice, bringing together specialists from several medical fields to better perform diagnoses and treatment.

June 30, 1971 – The 26th Amendment to the U.S. Constitution was enacted, granting the right to American citizens 18 years or older to vote. The minimum voting age in most states had been 21.

COMMENCEMENT

Early summer usually marks the end of a school year. On graduation days, celebrities of all kinds are invited to give commencement speeches at colleges and universities across the country. Some praiseworthy ones get quoted by the media and broadcasted to the world. In my humble opinion, no other profession deserves to praise its graduates more than those in healthcare. For not only do we have some of the longest and most arduous curricula, the end of our schooling is truly the beginning of our learning life.

We encounter thousands of people with countless problems, complaints, concerns, and questions. People reveal the most intimate and personal predicament to us - total strangers - and expect us to resolve them. Encounters and expectations are usually proper and within the realm of our training and experience. But they can also be unrealistic, comical, dim-witted, profane, and even devious. Yet we are asked to be impartial, professional, non-judgmental, unbiased, and helpful. A lot to ask from an individual, even with years of experience, never mind a novice or an inexpert. Still, there it is and we have to deal with it and not get burned in the process.

Along the way, the experience and knowledge we gain is priceless and thus behooves us to pass it on to others. Sharing this information enriches everyone, the student as well as the teacher. The more we share, the more we gain.

For indeed a beautiful gift given to us by life is experience.

Experience gives us understanding.

Understanding gives us knowledge.

Knowledge gives us know-how.

Know-how gives us satisfaction.

Satisfaction makes our lives happy.

Such is the wisdom of life.

Wise people have a fulfilled life.

ALLERGIES

In summer time as we venture outdoors, allergies and environmental reactions cause havoc on some of us. It is a malady many deal with on a regular basis. It is interesting that our advanced and modern medicine has not been able to eradicate this problem and if anything, our industrial world has drastically contributed and added to its challenges. Looking back on the history of allergies, we see that it has always been perplexing to the medical practitioners.

The earliest known report of an allergy was that of King Menses of Egypt, who died after a wasp sting around 3500 BC.

Roman philosopher Lucretius noted that "what is food for some may be fierce poison for others."

Shen Nong (c. 2700 BC) – considered the Father of Chinese Herbal Medicine – was the first to use ephedra to treat asthma-like symptoms five thousand years ago. While Frankincense, yellow ochre, and grapes were used to treat respiratory symptoms in Egypt around 3000-1200 BC.

Hippocrates (c. 460-377 BC) was one of the earliest physicians to understand the link between respiratory ailments and the environment.

The Talmud (Old Testament) discusses the use of hiltith, the Arabic word for asafetida, for prevention and treatment of asthma, whooping cough, and bronchitis.

Indian treatment of allergies like smoking stramonium for the treatment of asthma, was practiced by British army physicians for many years.

In the new world, dried root of the ipecacuanha which is a natural expectorant and balsam was used by Native Americans and taken back to Europe by Columbus and is used in cough medicines to this day. The ancient Americans also used ephedra and cocaine to treat rhinitis and asthma.

It's fascinating to note how remarkably advanced our ancient forefathers were in their understanding and treatment of allergies, yet the modern era of allergies didn't begin until the nineteenth century when hay fever was first described. Today many of the same challenges remain.

One reason may be that our medical profession keeps treating the symptoms rather than the root cause of the problem. Although the relationship of allergy and environment was realized thousands of years ago, our industrial age ignores all the evidence and pollutes our world with ever increasing harmful chemicals and substances. Every time the issue is brought up, the industry defends itself and denies any relationship by claiming that *their* scientists have found no correlations between the two.

As I mentioned earlier, in the late 1980s, I took a position in the West Texas city of Lubbock. The town sits among thousands of square miles of cotton and agricultural fields, as well as oil fields. The fields are routinely sprayed with insecticides and weed killers. Many toxic gases escape the thousands of oil wells. Soon after moving there, I developed joint inflammations and arthritic symptoms – similar to heavy metal poisoning. My wife too developed allergic symptoms of teary eyes, runny nose and slight wheezing. Our children also were overcome by allergy symptoms. When we sought medical help, a gamut of injections, medications and allergy symptom relief were prescribed. Not once did any of our providers mention that the very environment we lived in was causing the problem.

I had kept my practice back home in New Mexico and would spend several days a month working back home. I noticed that when I was home, my symptoms improved and I felt better. When my contract was up, we moved back to NM and soon after, our allergic symptoms subsided and resolved.

There are hundreds, if not thousands of towns nestled in agricultural fields all over this country and the world. The industrial age, population growth, demands for more food and necessities have placed people in contact with new allergens, thus we owe it to ourselves and our patients to be mindful of these interactions and potential harm they may cause us. At the least we need to make our patients aware of these potential threats. The new technologies at our disposal can educate us as well as our patients on these regards.

STORM WARNING

The howling wind outside the roadside restaurant kept us inside. There was a warning that the police may close the road. Looking around, about twenty or so travelers and locals were scattered throughout the establishment. The hour was late and the nearest town, sixty miles away. Weary eyes scan the sky for a break but none was coming. An old farmhand across the counter informed us that he had never seen it this bad. Talking persistently and asking; "Where are you from? Where are you going to? Tell me sir, are the people there better than me and you?"

Though he was inquisitive, no one seemed to care. The empty conversation was strangely welcomed. Once he learned that I was in healthcare, he first told me of his numerous aches and pains, then asked for advice and finally complained about not getting any help out here in the country.

"What am I doing here?" I asked myself. I was on my way to a clinic in the northeast part of New Mexico, when I got caught in the storm. The clinic's only provider had to leave on a family emergency and I was asked to cover for him.

"Why can't I say no?" I admonished myself. But I knew why! The cost is high for the people of this region. With no regular income or job, most depend on others. The local farms need the part-time workers. Without their help, they could not manage and people like me wouldn't get the produce we need.

"Where are you going to? Are the people there better than me and you?" The Old farmer went on asking another as the light of the day faded and customers' uneasiness increased. The proprietor wanted to go home but he himself was stuck by the storm.

Then just as suddenly as it had come, the wind stopped and the weather settled. Everyone dashed to their cars and as I was pulling away, I noticed the lights going out at the cafe as the owner left to go home.

The rest of my journey that evening was uneventful, but I could not help thinking of the last two hours of my life, and wondered where did the old farmer go?

Looking back, modern technology would have eliminated the need for my travel there. Yet that clinic, miles from the nearest hospital and city, today, still struggles to get providers to help them out. Much has changed since that encounter. Over the years, telehealth and telemedicine have become a reality, and many have done tremendous work with it, like UNM Project ECHO. Still others are abusing it. The storm of the recent pandemic was an eye-opener. It brought many changes to the world of business, work, education, and communication – healthcare included. But was it for better? A voice deep within me seems to whisper a warning that the old farmhand and the likes of him have not found a resolution to their predicament and that those in real need of this technology are not getting it.

FLAG, FATHER AND NOBEL

June 14 is Flag Day – the day (June 14, 1777) that marks the adoption of the flag of the United States by resolution of the Second Continental Congress.

Another day that we celebrate in June is Father's Day, to honor our fathers. Just as a flag raises the sense of patriotism in people, Fathers Day raises sense of responsibility, affection and devotion in all of us. These two days help us celebrate our civility and sense of belonging, to our families, country, beliefs, and our fellow man.

Unfortunately, the political rhetoric of some of the world leaders have left many to believe that to be patriotic is to harm those who do not agree with us. Obviously this strategy is not working and it may be a good time for us to rethink our approach to our problems. For, as Mahatma Gandhi said, "An eye for an eye will soon leave the whole world blind."

Sometimes, we have to go out of our way to execute the needed task. A good example of this can be seen in the work of peace activist and novelist Baroness Bertha von Suttner. Born on June 9th, 1843 in Prague. As a popular peace activist, her work was read overwhelmingly. Her book *Lay Down Your Arms (1889)* was well received. She traveled all over Europe and in her mid 30s became the secretary to the industrialist Alfred Nobel.

Nobel had made a fortune as the inventor of dynamite and later through the development of weapons. Bertha became an influencing factor on Nobel and convinced him to create what is now known as the Nobel Peace Prize. Nobel died in 1896, and the first Nobel Prize was given in 1901.

In 1905, Bertha von Suttner became the first woman to win the Nobel Peace Prize that she had helped create.

Today the need for peace and harmony is paramount. We, as healthcare providers, can be a catalyst in starting a spark to light the torch of hope and we have the tools to make our torch be seen far away. New communication tools can carry the light of our torch around the world. Let's make our flag be one of hope and peace!

LEARN, EXPERIENCE, TEACH

Marcus Tullius Cicero (106 BC – 43 BC), the great Roman politician said; "What greater or better gift can we offer the republic than to teach our youth?"

Indeed! There is no greater way for people to remember us than as a teacher, coach or mentor. For in the practice of healthcare, every encounter teaches us something about humanity as well as medicine. Sharing that knowledge with our students and colleagues – young and old – should be the goal of us all.

Our first job out of medical school is the one we will never forget. Those of us lucky enough will land a job in a busy clinic, hospital or private practice where other experienced practitioners and providers are at hand to help guide and mentor us. Others may find themselves in situations where such resources are limited or non-existent. Personally, I feel that two years of work at a large hospital should be mandatory, though some argue that the residency provides that experience – I disagree.

But no matter the situation, we are all learning on the job (OJT) and the most important thing will be good communication. Successful communication occurs when others contribute meaningfully to your decision. It does not occur when you assume a despotic posture. Even if the consultation is inadequate, it may shine a light on alternative possibilities of diagnosing, deciding and treating. Sometimes even a small familiarity can save the day. Once while working at an urgent-care, my shift started late in the morning. I arrived at work and noticed the waiting room to be full. As I walked to the back, I saw that all four of my colleagues working that day had their heads buried in different medical books searching for something. Approaching the nurses' station, I saw a large canning jar with something in it on the counter. I picked it up and with astonishment called out; "Ascaris? Where did this come from?"

Four heads rose from the books and turned to me. One asked; "Is that what that is?"

"Yes" I answered, "where did it come from?"

He pointed to a young man in an exam room. He was from Central America here visiting family when he got sick and started passing the parasites in his stool. Mystery solved and everyone went back to work. In my times of working in the Caribbean and Middle East, I had seen and treated many infested by such vermin. It wasn't that I was smarter than the others, I just had a bit of diversity in my experience.

Not long ago, I came across an article on Virtual Veterinary Training that was established by Tufts University Veterinary School. It connected with veterinarians in Africa, allowing Tufts students to experience caring for large African animals. I wrote about it in a newsletter I was writing for a telehealth organization and it received some attention, not because of our readers' interest in veterinary medicine, but rather due to a knowledge it provided for Tufts' students that they would have otherwise not been able to get.

Today, more than ever, our world needs good and experienced healthcare providers. The ever changing mixture and diversity of our communities demands knowledge of problems or situations that was not expected of us to face, so it was not taught to us in school. But economics, natural disasters, famine, wars, political changes, all have placed average communities and people in dire situations where their health has been affected and getting care, more difficult. We may find ourselves caring for cultures we know nothing about. In times like this our new technologies can close the gap. Whether novice or experienced, we can all use some help at times. And when we learn it, it behooves us to pass it on and teach others. As Bernard Shaw said; "I am not a teacher: only a fellow-traveler of whom you asked the way. I pointed ahead – ahead of myself as well as you."

JULY

Of note in July

July 1, 1862 – President Abraham Lincoln signed the first income tax bill. Then by the act of Congress, the Bureau of Internal Revenue was established on this day.

July 2, 1964 – President Lyndon B. Johnson signed the Civil Rights Act of 1964, prohibiting discrimination on the basis of race in public accommodations, publicly owned or operated facilities, employment and union membership and in voter registration.

July 4, 1776 – The Declaration of Independence was approved by the Continental Congress.

July 6, 1885 – Louis Pasteur gave the first successful anti-rabies inoculation to a boy who had been bitten by an infected dog.

July 9, 1868 – The 14th Amendment to the U.S. Constitution was ratified. The Amendment defined U.S. citizenship and prohibited individual States from abridging the rights of any American citizen without due process and equal protection under the law. The Amendment also barred individuals involved in rebellion against the U.S. from holding public office.

July 12, 1997 – It's the birthday of Malala Yousafzai from Pakistan, the youngest Nobel Peace Prize winner – and at 17, the youngest Nobel Prize winner in any category.

July 13, 1787 – Congress enacted the Northwest Ordinance (its worthwhile to look this up)

July 18, 1947 – President Harry Truman signed an Executive Order determining the line of succession if the president becomes incapacitated or dies in office. Following the vice president, the speaker of the house and president of the Senate are next in succession. This became the 25th Amendment to the U.S. Constitution, ratified on February 10, 1967.

July 19, 1799 – French soldiers in Napoleon's army discovered the Rosetta Stone.

July 20, 1969 – Apollo 11 Astronaut Neil Armstrong took his first step on the moon and proclaimed; "That's one small step for man, one giant leap for mankind". The event was broadcast on television and watched around the world.

July 22, 1822 – It is the birthday of the Moravian natural scientist and meteorologist Johann Gregor Mendel, born in Czechoslovakia. From 1856 to 1863, he performed experiments on 28,000 edible pea plants. From his observations, he developed his theory of inheritance, including the notion of recombination of genes, which became the basis of the modern science of genetics.

IT IS A SMALL WORLD

Fourth of July is America's independence day and our birthday. Happy birthday America! It is interesting to note that 21 other countries celebrate their independence in July as well. Yet despite the fact that many proudly commemorate their autonomy, the business world unites and tears down barriers.

A family member who has traveled extensively throughout Southeast Asia told of a time she was traveling the northern regions of Borneo in Malaysia. She was on a train to Tenom Station and passing through the jungle, marveling at the scenery and relatively simple way of life. She was hungry by the time the train reached the station and thinking of where to eat when, to her astonishment, she saw a sign for Pizza Hut next to the station. I was Googling the map to follow her trip and sure enough there is a Pizza Hut and a KFC in Tenom, which shows the globalization of our commerce and businesses.

When serving on the board of a Telehealth group, we received a request from a medical student in South Korea who, enthusiastically wanted to introduce Korean medicine – the complementary medicine in Korea – to the world using telemedicine. We informed him that there are active telemedicine programs in South Korea, commonly called "ubiquitous Health" (uHealth) and that he had the opportunity to visit with some of the key stakeholders in Seoul. We further informed him that the integration of traditional healing is a common theme in many countries around the world.

It was different in a not so distance past. In 1972, biologist David Werner, working in the mountains of Western Mexico, wrote the book *Donde no hay doctor* (Where There Is No Doctor) in Spanish for the village healthcare workers. In an interview in 2009 with the Japanese Society for Rehabilitation of Persons with Disabilities (JSRPD), he said that in Mexican villages, the people would choose the person they wanted to become a village health worker. Someone that really cared about other people and had some skills to offer and willingness to learn and to give of themselves. But there was no good educational material to teach them proper healthcare techniques, so he wrote this sort of manual in simple language. The book became very popular and has been translated into many languages – including English. Much of what the book covers is the old and traditional ways of healthcare practices incorporated into modern methods.

Likewise in 1977, the Official Chinese Paramedical Manual of *A Barefoot Doctor's Manual* was translated into English and became popular and taught us many Chinese traditional medicine practices – many of which were thought of as archaic, barbaric or nonsense by the western educated practitioners. Yet many of these old world techniques have been found to have sound application so much so that they now have standard application in our practice, like acupuncture, massage therapy and even use of leaches and maggots.

Back then these books had to be purchased and any concerns or questions were hard to address by the authors. Today's technology, not only brings this information to us but addresses and answers inquiries in a very timely fashion helping the student and educator alike.

Many practitioners practicing telemedicine travel the world promoting telehealth, from the jungles of South America to the Middle East and Southeast Asia. It is amazing how a rare disease in a remote village up the Amazon River can be treated directly by university doctors, 4000 miles away. And how I can write about it while listening to Flamingo music performed in Barcelona, Spain. It is indeed a small world after all.

Our technology connects us in ways not perceivable even a few short years ago. We can reach out and touch each other across the world, help one another, treat diseases, advise on social, economic and commercial matters. Even attend scientific and trade meetings on the other side of the country or enjoy a live concert thousands of miles away without having to leave our home base. But there are still places that lack this connection and it's remarkable that some actually resist it – on both sides. But if we can sell American style pizza and chicken around the world, we can share our knowledge of medicine and healthcare with others. Teach as well as learn from one another. Let us be one of those who remove barriers rather than raise them.

Let's not forget that we declared our independence with these words: "We hold these truths to be self-evident, that all men are created equal, that they are endowed by their Creator with certain unalienable Rights, that among these are Life, Liberty and the pursuit of Happiness, ..."

Perhaps the right to Good Healthcare should have also been included.

IMMIGRANTS PLIGHT

"There is a baby with a rash outside in a car," the nurse informed me one day long ago. "Will you go and check it out?"

It was our policy to keep children with a rash out of the urgent care – where I worked – to prevent spreading it to others. Warning placards, in Spanish and English, were placed at the entrance to alert patients that we would come out and see the patient and not to bring them in.

"Buenos Dias." I said in my accented and limited Spanish and continued to inquire about the nature of the rash covering a very young infant's body. It turned out to be a garden variety children's viral disease and not one of the dreaded ones like measles. What makes me remember the case was not the baby's illness, but rather the distraught state of the mother. She was visibly scared, looking around at every car passing by. I looked at my interpreter questioningly.

"She is undocumented and worried about the cops." She whispered in my ear. The morning news had reported that there was a big raid the night before and many undocumented migrants were arrested by the INS. Apparently some of her family members were among the arrested. I prescribed the usual treatment for the baby and they left in a hurry.

I could not get the mother out of my mind for a long time that day. For despite the great danger she felt in being discovered, she sought help for her sick baby. We prevented the baby from spreading his infection to others in our waiting area but were sure that the cramped and poor conditions of the residences of these migrants did not prevent the spread to others in their community. After all, that was probably how her baby contracted the infection. Although I did ask about others being sick, her alarmed reaction to my inquiry about others made it clear that no proper response would be coming as she was ready to bolt out of there.

The incident happened many years ago, yet today we are further from resolving this problem than ever before. This article was written in July, when we celebrate our independence day. Two hundred forty years ago, we said no to tyranny, control and prejudice. Our very motto of freedom became; "Give me your tired, your poor, your huddled masses yearning to breathe free, The wretched refuse of your teeming shore. Send these, the homeless, tempest-tossed, to me: I lift my lamp beside the golden door."

The anti-immigrant fervor today however, is doing the opposite and closing all doors to these very people. Argument on the legality or right or wrongness of the issues aside, what do we do when as healthcare professionals we are asked to care for these people. In medicine, we are trained to give care to all who need it. Despite any racial, geopolitical, or other discriminating or prejudicial status. But how do you treat fear, uncertainty, despondency, or need.

Today we do have tools like telemedicine and tele-education to help many near and far. But the use of these tools themselves, have become controversial and contentious. Turf control, financial consideration and political misunderstandings are limiting the use of these wonderful tools. Maybe these technologies are advancing too fast, but so are the plight and need of millions of hungry, poor refugees all around the world. Let's put our racial, geopolitical, discriminating prejudices aside and help people. Let's live up to our motto. Even if we don't want these masses to come here, we can take help to them through our technology.

WOMEN OF MEDICINE

It is said that Ginger Rogers did everything Fred Astaire did but backwards and in high heels. Which proves that many of our female counterparts are much stronger than we give them credit for. Whether the masculine part of humanity likes it or not, this is true intellectually as well as physically. But it is a shame that they have to struggle to prove it.

In the medical profession, women have contributed enormously. Many were of Latin heritage. *Dr. Helen Rodriguez-Trias* – whose birthday was July 7, 1929 (Dec. 27, 2001) – was one such person (its worthwhile to look up her history). Trías completed her medical studies at the University of Puerto Rico earning her degree in 1960. She accomplished much in her life that has had a lasting effect in medicine to this day. She spent much of her medical career in Puerto Rico and New York. In 1974, she was revolutionizing the way women of color were being treated in this country. She took up practice at Lincoln Hospital in South Bronx, NY. At that time it so happened that I was going through my own residency at that hospital. Although – I am sorry to say – that I don't recall having crossed paths with her, I am sure that we did.

She helped expand public health services for women and children in minority and low-income populations around the world including the first center for the care of newborn babies in Puerto Rico. She was the first president of the American Public Health Association (APHA) of Latina decent and the recipient of the Presidential Citizens Medal – awarded to her by

President Bill Clinton. New York City has built a statue honoring Rodríguez Trías in St. Mary's Park, near Lincoln Hospital in the Bronx.

Rodríguez Trías said: "We need health, but above all we need to create a grounding for healthy public policy that redresses and salvages the growing inequities. We cannot achieve a healthier us without achieving a healthier, more equitable health care system, and ultimately, a more equitable society."

Another Latina doctor that I *do* remember very well, as she was instrumental in my decision to stay in the medical field, was Dr. Angela Ramirez. Also a female Puerto Rican physician. She was going through residency at Elmhurst General Hospital in NY in the 1963–66 time frame. I was a nineteen year old tech working in the ER. I did most of the x-ray development and casting of the patients. She was a surgical resident and appreciated the understanding of medicine that I had learned from my years of working in surgery back in my home country and by watching the many doctors treating the patients in our very busy ER.

November 9, 1965 was a night I will never forget. Due to a glitch, the entire North Eastern US lost electrical power right in the middle of the rush hour. This New York City blackout was devastating and costly. Our hospital was affected as well and although we had a backup generator, somehow no one could get it to work. No power meant no x-ray, no elevators, no OR lights, nothing. Many of the injured had lacerations and other injuries that needed immediate care. Dr. Ramirez was the surgical resident on call that night. Flashlights in hand, I helped her suture many of these patients. Her cool and composed demeanor calmed the patients and helped us deal with the very demanding situations. We worked all through the night and well into the next day. She was very encouraging and under flashlights and the chaos around us, explained what she was doing and even let me put in a few sutures – my first real ones in the new world.

After her residency she moved back to Puerto Rico and I was drafted and entered the United States Air Force and moved to Texas. We lost contact but I never forgot her. Years later, I met a member of the Puerto Rican Medical Board at a national conference who knew Angela Ramirez and told me that she had settled in Mayagüez but was in very poor health. I wrote her a long letter and tried to make contact but never heard back. I fear that we have lost a very good doctor and educator. Many more doctors like Trias and Ramirez have contributed to our profession. We salute you and thank you for all your contribution and devotion.

NOTHING NEW

In considering our world, I find it amazing that millions of people of all races and nationalities all have the same simple and similar wishes, hopes, desires and needs. We all have one set of eyes and ears, a mouth, two hands and a brain. Yet our hands, guided by eyes and controlled by the mind can craft magnificent objects, paint emotions, grow crops, play music, tighten screws on a bike, bridge or an ocean liner. Our eyes can gaze at the stars, read a book, stare down a microscope, glance at that passing beauty and even weep for a loss. Millions of talents with so many potentials and possibilities, only if given an equal chance. I don't think anyone is worth more than anyone else!

Disparities can wreck havoc on a soul and discourage even the most devoted. Whether one is lost in a bottle, smoke or a syringe, finding the way into clarity is easier said than done. When the only means of income is leftover coins in a payphone or on the sidewalk and after your family is murdered, your home burned, your very existence ripped apart, it is hard to understand why your rich neighbor – who knows you– won't lend a hand. Its not that many of us don't care, rather it is because we have become numb to what surrounds us. But there is nothing new about this.

In Florence, Italy stands Piazza della Repubblica, a nineteen-century reconstruction of the old city. On the west side of the plaza stands the porticos with the triumphal arch, called the "Arcone". On the top of the Arcane, an ostentatious inscription reads:

L'ANTICO CENTRO DELLA CITTÀ
DA SECOLARE SQUALLORE
A VITA NUOVA RESTITUITO

(The ancient center of the city / restored from age-old squalor / to new life)

Apparently the city center of Florence became home to the homeless and transients who abused it. The city fathers then decided to run everyone out, demolish and rebuild a wider and modern plaza, with the above dedication.

Sound familiar? Today too, many major cities around the world face the same problem with the homeless, poor, and unemployed members of their society. But instead of solving the underlying civil failure of their community, they chase the unfortunate out and spend money restoring the area that eventually will attract new groups of the same.

Regrettably the political atmosphere of our world is polarizing people and our wonderful communication technology isolates us further. The ever increasing poverty in many parts of the world forcing many to migrate for economic reasons thus making it more difficult to separate the needy from the political refugees. All of which makes the work of healthcare providers more challenging yet urgent. Luckily, many of our colleagues provide for the needy around the world while avoiding all the political hot air. Many of them work with and employ telecommunication into their practice and are part of an international healthcare organization that brings help to the needy around the world. I have worked with many of them and appreciate their hard work. It is indeed a daunting task, especially when they have to fight the many bureaucracies restricting their efforts.

HISTORY IS A MIRROR

All over the southwestern states, the owners of the land came onto the land, or more often, someone came for them. All of the owners told their tenants the same thing: 'You know the land's getting poorer. The bank has to have profits all the time. It can't wait for the next year's crops. One man on a tractor can take the place of twelve or fourteen families. You'll have to go.'

Then the tractors came over the roads and into the fields. They drove through fences and houses to make space for even larger fields.

Grapes of Wrath by John Steinbeck.

We all remember the story. We read it in high school. It was required reading. It still is! Those folks were pushed off their home, land, even state and country and we should recall the terrible welcome awaiting them elsewhere. Many died on their exodus and many more arrived sick and injured.

Today hundreds of thousands of our citizens are destitute and homeless. Many have become so depressed and helpless they have succumbed to drugs, alcohol, even suicide. So much so that our country is facing an unprecedented tragedy.

In Middle American states like Kentucky, West Virginia, Tennessee and others, the middle age white man's rate of death has increased by over three hundred percent. Most deaths are due to drugs, alcoholism, and suicide. A CDC report indicates that the rate from suicide or unintentional death due to substance abuse has increased dramatically in recent years. The tragedy is not just the loss of these people but often that of the family they leave behind. A new increasing problem is the fate of numerous children left parentless. Many seniors suddenly find themselves having to care for their very young grandchildren.

A recent report from Brookings Institution by Ann Case and the Nobel laureate; Sir Angus Deaton, reveals the tremendous burden to our society, these "Deaths of despair" are creating.

But are we missing something? There are nearly seventy million displaced people around the world. The majority are in much worse predicament than any of us. Yet in many cases the suicide rate among them is lower than ours. Many Europeans too have suffered in these economic upheavals, but the percentage of the suicide rate of many is lower. The refugee population shows families staying together, even in their plight of leaving their homeland. During the great depression too, families were close. When the going got bad, families coalesced and helped each other to keep moving. So, is today's family structure a problem or are we looking at something entirely different? No matter what the problem though, when depression sets in, many will turn to their family healthcare providers for help. A lot of us are ill equipped and not trained to deal with this dilemma and may overlook the basic principle underlying this conundrum. How we treat them will determine whether we solve or add to the overall harm of the crisis.

One caveat is the technology at our disposal. Using technology to provide help can drastically reduce the burden of dealing with the intricacies of the dilemma. Especially to our colleagues in rural areas where the problem seems to be ever more acute and at times hopeless. As more information becomes available, we can rapidly educate ourselves and our colleagues through these tools. Maybe we can't replace the family support or resolve the underlying economical and social obstacles but we *can* educate ourselves properly and provide solace by showing that we care!

FIFA

During the games of the World Cup in 2018, like millions of people around the world, I was glued to the TV watching the World Cup's final game between France and Croatia. The game was amazing and so was the commercial value of it.

The contagiousness of watching a sport game is universal. Different cultures and nations have their favorites, but the ubiquitous excitement they feel for it is unmistakably similar. Baseball, American Football, the Olympics' national competitions, boxing matches, sumo wrestling and others are a testament to the power of sport's attraction.

Of course, what makes it such a success is the teamwork that goes into it. The entire community or sometimes even the nation contributes to that teamwork. Business and people's participation at the games supports a multi-billion dollar tourism industry of its own. Why so many people will travel long distances to join others in watching their favorite game is mind-boggling.

Traveling through the Baltimore area once, I stopped at a roadside motel to rest for the night, only to be told that they had no vacancy. "Could you tell me where is the nearest hotel *with* a vacancy?" I asked the proprietor.

"You can try Philadelphia, or Washington!" was the answer.

He laughed at my surprise and said; "Preakness is in town, you are not going to find an empty room anywhere in the Baltimore area this weekend."

"What's Preakness?" I asked clueless.

"The horse races!" he said with astonishment at my ignorance.

I slept in my car in the parking lot of a Highway Howard Johnson that night. I was not alone.

I had a similar experience of sleeping in my car outside of Brands Hatch in Kent, England, during formula car races and a friend tells of the time she and her husband had to camp out in the local park while traveling through Aguascalientes, Mexico, during the Bullfighting competition week. Likewise, an uninformed traveler can expect to use the car as sleeping room the first week of October in Albuquerque, NM, during the Balloon Fiesta.

Now just think how wonderful a world we could have if we got this excited about our healthcare. Even a little excitement would add to the well being of us all, and with all the technology available to us, it would be at a fraction of the cost of establishing, providing and participating in these national pastimes.

Of course, I realize that it is the competitiveness of sports that make them so exciting and providing healthcare is not a competitive sport. But it does require and demand teamwork. That teamwork could be built upon. The world around us seems to be unraveling at an alarming rate. We may not be able to change it, but as healthcare providers, we can assure that the service we provide *is* to the best of our ability. And showing a little enthusiasm in providing it well could be contagious.

THE MAGICIAN
HAD NO HANDS

The magician had no hands. As a matter of fact he had just a semblance of a limb on the right and upper stump of an arm on the left. Yet he expertly shuffled the cards and spread them on the table, as he continued to delight, fascinate and mesmerize the audience on live TV. As he finished his spell-binding show, he stepped down from the platform, he was standing on and struggled to carry his four feet tall dwarfed body off the stage – the audience, enthralled and impressed, cheering and roaring enthusiastically. At that moment he was king, smiling ear-to-ear and bowing happily. His handicapped body did not enter into the equation at all. The show was not about his physical ability; rather it was about his magical prowess. The audience shook their heads and asked each other how the magic was done rather than how he could have done the magic.

Years ago, while standing on a street corner in New Delhi, India, I watched a young man with a badly deformed body twist, rotate and contort himself into unbelievable positions. But unlike our magician on stage, the Indian audience of our street magician watched with indifference and only a few threw coins his way. As a healthcare provider, I not only watched the magician on stage with gaiety, but also wondered about all the health and medical issues he has to deal with on a daily basis. He however seemed well nourished and otherwise healthy, despite his handicap. The poor wretch of a young man I witnessed in India though, was anything but healthy. Many bruises, cuts and skin lesions were a testament to his destitute existence. The contrast between these examples reveals the many disparities among citizens of this world. Though both were physically handicapped, the comparison ended there.

It is easy to blame their circumstances on socio-political aspects of their respective societies; it does not however alleviate the unjust and insufferable condition of one over the other.

The fact that many such disparities exist in our world is saddening. But it is even more heartbreaking to know that it really does not take much to bring help and relief of pain to many of our fellow men. Especially today with the magnificent technology available to us, we really could make a difference. And we don't have to go to the other side of the world to find people in need. Many in our own rural and under-served communities could use our help.

BEATING CANCER

A few years back, a CBS program; "Sunday Morning" was devoted entirely to cancer. Hosted by Dr. Jon LaPook, it showed the progress being made in understanding, research, and the treatment options of this dreaded disease.

One common problem is the continuous lack of true and timely communication between researchers and the application of their findings. The main hurdle seems to be the bureaucratic obstacles put in place by regulatory agencies.

The CBS report showed the advancement made by major cancer hospitals and institutions such as Memorial Sloan Kettering Cancer Center in NY, John Hopkins in Baltimore, and Seattle Cancer Care Alliance of The University of Washington Medical Center. Many others, too, are making groundbreaking and advanced progress in this arena here and internationally. Clearly this is a much needed yet daunting task. So it stands to reason that cooperation of all involved would benefit everyone.

Access to patients needing treatment, is always difficult. Especially in the area of rare diseases (see the article; *"Telehealth and Leprosy, BBS and Stroke"* in the April section). It is overwhelming for some patients to travel to a center away from home for treatment, since many cannot afford to travel to far away cities for care. Even if the cost of treatment is covered by insurance or some grant, family members cannot leave home to stay with their loved ones during the often long periods of treatment. Loss of income and family support adds to the anxiety and pain of having to deal with a relative's fight with his/her disease.

It's not just major problems like cancer that create hardship and unnecessary expense. Sometimes even a minor and relatively small medical issue could cause harm when ignorant pride takes control. A PA colleague tells a story of a patient she once saw at a resort clinic she was working at. A new provider in town was setting up office and trying to impress the small town populous. A visitor to the resort had developed a rather sever conjunctivitis and was seen by the PA. She started him on ophthalmic antibiotic and had him return the next day for follow-up. She was late getting to work the next day and the patient went to see the other provider, who became alarmed by the severity of the infection and being new to the area, figured that the nearest ophthalmologist must be in the nearest city, 110 miles away. He patched the now alarmed patient's eye and instructed him to travel there for immediate care, less he might lose the eye.

The out of town visitor had come with a church group on a bus. He had to find an expensive ride to take him to the far away city. They passed two small towns on the way – one 40 miles away and another 80 miles away with an ophthalmologist on their staff. In the big city, the patient – being a walk-in, had to wait a long time to be seen. When he was finally seen by the doctor, was told that he indeed had a severe conjunctivitis and to continue with the given medication by the PA and follow-up with his family doctor on return home. The understandably irate patient returned to the resort town late that night. The next day, well you can imagine what happened next.

A simple phone call could have lessened the trauma and had Internet and telehealth been available then, he could have saved the patient a trip altogether.

In the case of the cancer patients, we all know is that treating them in their home environment is preferable to dislocating them for the sake of an experimental method that may or may not work – as usually is the case with investigational approaches. Many local cancer centers are equipped to handle the long-term hospitalization needed for these patients. If regulatory agencies allow specialists from major institutions to treat patients at their home centers without having unrealistic demands, much advancement could be made in beating cancer. Cost too, could be shared if doctors of several institutions cooperate and treat patients at other locations without having to be licensed in every state or center. This could easily be done by the new communication tools.

The Federation of the State Medical Boards and many medical associations have been working for years on resolving this issue. Progress is being made but is much too slow for many. A lot of hardship is tolerated by those stricken by cancer; bureaucratic hurdles should not be one of them.

FIRE AND STORM

The morning mist hugged the face of the mountain, magnifying its hills and valleys. It was surreal as the rays of the morning sun found its way through the jagged peaks and the mist. The high altitude temperature of the Rockies was comfortable, but with a hint that it was going to get very hot later in the day. Back in the house, the morning news revealed a frightening map of the world on fire. Wildfires burning across the Western US, Central America, Asia, Europe, Australia, and Africa. No continent seemed to be spared. Where there were no fires, rain, floods, hurricanes, tornados or typhoons causing mayhem. Global Warming is fully at work and moving to change the very face of our planet. Yet there are those who claim that mankind has no control over the weather therefore is not responsible for its affect. Like ostriches, they would rather stick their heads in the sand than face the reality of it. There actually was a cartoon in the New Yorker that portrayed members in a boardroom doing just that.

Many seem to have the same sentiment about healthcare. Arguing that illness and sickness are part of life, therefore governments can't be held responsible. The barriers one faces in asking for affordable healthcare is always fighting for a budget and trying to justify and convince people about the importance of a healthy society. It's like fighting for flood control and fire prevention when everything is fine. But it is not till the water is filling the living room or fire rushing across the fence into the yard that we wish the provisions were there.

Today technology is making it easier for us to reach many, but availability of that technology to everyone around the world is costly. Still with a little help, we can provide healthcare affordably and profitably. We have the knowledge and we have the tools, so with a little foresight we can navigate away from the fires and storm.

AUGUST

Of note in August

August 1, 1779 (1843) – Francis Scott Key was born in Frederick County, Maryland. After seeing the American flag still flying over Fort McHenry, following the British attack the day before (September 13, 1814), he wrote a poem entitled "Defense of Fort McHenry", which became our National Anthem (The Star-Spangled Banner) in 1931.

August 2, 1776 – The Continental Congress signed the Declaration of Independence in Philadelphia.

August 2, 1939 – Albert Einstein informed President Franklin D. Roosevelt concerning the possibility of atomic weapons. He wrote; "A single bomb of this type carried by boat and exploded in a port, might very well destroy the whole port together with some of the surrounding territory."

August 3, 1492 – Christopher Columbus set sail from Palos, Spain, with three ships, *Nina, Pinta* and *Santa Maria*. He landed in the Bahamas on October 12th.

August 4, 1901 (1971) – Louis Armstrong (Satchmo) was born in New Orleans, Louisiana.

August 5, 1861 – President Abraham Lincoln signed the first Federal income tax law, a 3 percent tax on incomes over $800.

August 6-10, 1787 – The Constitutional Convention established a four-year term of office for the President, granting Congress the right to regulate foreign trade and interstate commerce.

August 6, 1881 (1955) – Alexander Fleming was born in Lochfield, Scotland. He discovered Penicillin and received the Nobel Prize in 1954.

August 6, 1945 – The first Atomic Bomb was dropped over Hiroshima.

August 6, 1965 – The Voting Rights Act was signed into law by President Lyndon B. Johnson. The Act suspended literacy, knowledge and character tests designed to keep African-Americans from voting.

August 9, 1945 – The second atomic bomb was dropped over Nagasaki.

August 13, 1927 – Cuban President Fidel Castro was born in Mayari, Oriente Province, Cuba.

August 14, 1935 – President Roosevelt signed the Social Security Act.

August 14, 1941 – The Atlantic Charter was issued by President Franklin D. Roosevelt and British Prime Minister Winston Churchill. The Charter, a foundation for the establishment of the United Nations, set forth eight goals for the nations of the world, including; the renunciation of all aggression, right to self-government, access to raw materials, freedom from want and fear, freedom of the seas, and disarmament of aggressor nations.

August 14, 1945 – VJ Day, Japan surrendered to the Allies.

August 15-18, 1969 – Woodstock happened in upstate N.Y.

August 17, 1978 – The first transatlantic balloon trip was completed by Max Anderson, Ben Abruzzo, and Larry Newman, all from Albuquerque, New Mexico. They launched from Maine on August 11th, in *Double Eagle II* and traveled about 3,000 miles in 137 hours, landing about 60 miles west of Paris.

August 18, 1920 – The 19th Amendment to the U.S. Constitution was ratified, granting women the right to vote.

August 19, 1871 (1948) – Aviation pioneer Orville Wright (1871–1948) was born in Dayton, Ohio.

August 21, 1959 – Hawaii became the 50th state.

August 24, 1572 – Thousands of Protestant Huguenots were massacred in Paris and throughout France by Catholics, in what became known as the St. Bartholomew's Day Massacre.

August 26, 1883 – One of the most catastrophic volcanic eruptions in recorded history occurred on the Indonesian island of Krakatoa. Explosions were heard 2,000 miles away. Tidal waves 120 ft. high killed 36,000 people and five cubic miles of earth were blasted into the air up to a height of 50 miles.

August 26, 1910 (1997) – Mother Teresa was born (as Agnes Gonxha Bojaxhiu) in Skopje, Yugoslavia. She founded a religious order of nuns in Calcutta, India, called the Missionaries of Charity.

August 29, 1632 (1704) – Philosopher John Locke was born in Wrington, England. His ideas that "Rulers derive their power only from the consent of the governed – and that men naturally possess certain rights, including life, liberty and property", greatly influenced the American colonists.

August 29, 1809 (1894) – Physician and author Oliver Wendell Holmes was born in Cambridge, Massachusetts. He once wrote, "A moment's insight is sometimes worth a life's experience."

August 29, 1991 – The Soviet Communist Party was suspended, ending the institution that ruled Soviet Russia for nearly 75 years.

ADOPT A RURAL HOSPITAL/ CLINIC

"One sometimes finds what one is not looking for." said Sir Alexander Fleming who was born on August 6th, 1881. He became a bacteriologist who discovered penicillin in 1928.

On the road to see my son who was getting married I noticed the "Adopt a highway" signs that ask organizations and community groups to adopt and care for a section of that highway and keep it clean. Such signs are seen on all US highways and roads. It occurred to me that it would be a great idea to have major medical centers, hospitals and schools adopt a rural hospital or clinic, in similar fashion. Bring them under their umbrella and see to their care and success. Many such arrangements are in the works right now but it usually is to send interns and residents to these rural community clinics on rotational basis. Although this is great, it benefits the rural communities minimally.

Our rural clinics and hospitals deserve more than just receiving students. They deserve a full-fledged support system. By every major medical institution adopting a rural health center, state of the art healthcare could be brought to these areas to the benefit of everyone. I am sure that legal minds and bean counters can find all kinds of ways to bring revenue to the majors through this support system, and in the process, real, timely, and proper care is provided to our rural communities. Let's adopt our rural hospitals and clinics and provide them the support system they deserve.

DUALITIES

The early morning light cleared the mountain ridge to slit through the curtains and welcome itself into my day. It was exhilarating to be awakened such. My wife had the radio on in the kitchen and Edvard Grieg's "Peer Gynt Suite" was playing softly. A perfect accompaniment for such a morning. I peeled the covers off and stood with sunshine in my face. Such blessing and beauty sent my way – overwhelming! The morning news though, was anything but pleasant. It portrayed a world in chaos, pain and despair. The contrast between my world and that, minutes or hours away was so profound that no amount of rationalization, philosophizing, or finger pointing for that matter, justified it.

I dressed and headed to town and our monthly healthcare board meeting. On the long drive there, I repeatedly changed the channels on the radio in the hope of hearing any news to compliment the sunshine of my morning. But it was not to be; even the traffic report was depressing. Finally, I settled on listening to the classical channel's music interrupted by screaming salesmen peddling their goods.

Our meeting discussed the many requests for assistance, our financial shortcomings and the many ideas we had on how to move healthcare forward and help people near and far. It gives me a glimmer of hope that at least we are making a difference in bringing healthcare to some rural parts of our world by pointing a few of our colleagues in the right direction.

The meeting concluded, errands done, chores accomplished, I headed home at the end of the day. The late afternoon clouds over the Sandia Mountain were ablaze in golden sunset. I kept the radio on classical and ignored the commercials. My wife handed me a cup of hot tea on my arrival. Sitting on the porch, I watched the last rays of the light draining from the cloud tops and the crickets announcing the coming of the night. With tears in my eyes, I counted my blessings and wished for a better tomorrow for all. For, this Escher(ian) duality of our world is, at the least, confusing – (See CULTURAL CONNECTIONS in the next section). But while some stab at the fabrics of our society with daggers and spears, many more of us are at hand with simple needle and thread sewing it back up.

CLINICS AND WALMART

News comes to us that Walmart is pushing forward with it's "a medical clinic in every store" concept, as Walgreen talks about expanding their pharmacy services to provide family healthcare to their customers. All, of course are planning to depend heavily on telehealth.

Although the use of telehealth and telemedicine is most appropriate and welcomed, one must question the commercialization of the concept. It is no secret that these organizations are very much "for profit" establishments. Thus it is a given that they will fully exploit their in-store clinics for profit. How they perform their task needs close scrutiny. Medicine is one art where close provider/ patient relationship is of paramount importance in good healthcare delivery. If these stores offer their healthcare services much like they do their bakery goods – roast the chicken and place it in the middle of an aisle for people to serve themselves – there will be problems. Providers at many of these businesses are routinely changed or rotated between branches. It seems, for example, that every time I go to my pharmacy at the local one of these stores, I find a new pharmacist working there. Often, I am told that the previous pharmacist is working at another store today. This practice makes it difficult to establish any rapport with one's provider, harming the very basic concept of practicing good medicine. And what about the medication prescribed? Will the patient receive the proper drug or one that the store has special contracts with? I can go on about many of such scenarios but I think that the message is clear.

On the other hand, the recent pandemic and the mandatory cancellation of social interactions and closure of businesses, including many medical clinics, hospital services and doctor offices forced much of our work to be done remotely and by way of telehealth, telemedicine and similar means. This event proved the efficacy of the idea of tele-work and the future proper use of the concept would be most welcomed and maybe the answer to the healthcare provider shortages of the twenty- first century, especially for our rural areas. We will just have to wait and see, but we must be ready to step in and correct things before they get away from us. Still that may be easier said than done – we must be vigilant.

OF CYCLONES, TYPHOONS, AND HURRICANES

The emptiness in the faces of the people was a testament to the suffering they had endured, reported a colleague with the Red Cross who arrived on the island in early September. Many sat staring into a distant void. Bruises on the faces and bodies, a tribute to what was witnessed. The air reeked of death with destruction permeating all senses. A warm gentle breeze swayed the broken palm trees, many harboring bits and pieces of things thrown at them earlier. The hood of a car wrapped around one tree, thirty feet high. Sheet metal roofing and building materials replaced what was once branches, leaves and flowers.

Hurricane David hit the island of Dominica on August 29, 1979. From there it traveled north to the Dominican Republic, the Bahamas, Florida, and up the US coastline.

In 1984, Dominica was still in disarray, needing help. Direct Relief International – an aid organization was asking for volunteers to the island, so I signed up. In April, I left Taos, NM and spent three months on the island. Though the hurricane had left four years earlier, the devastation was still there and the surmounting need for help very present. I got to see the damage these monster storms can do first hand and will never forget.

Since then many cyclones, typhoons, and hurricanes have ravaged our planet. No country in the world has been more devastated by these storms than the nation of Bangladesh. The mostly low-lying terrain is divided by the Ganges, Padma, Brahmaputra and about 700 other rivers, which empty into the Bay of Bengal. Of the ten deadliest storms in history, seven were in Bangladesh. The most recent was the Cyclone Mora that hit the country in May of 2017.

Though the structural damages are what we see and record, it is the human toll in these instances that are lasting. The loss of a family member is exceptional. So are the damages inflicted on human bodies and souls. Our profession sees this first hand. We are the first they call on, and when we get there, expectations are overwhelming and demand often unattainable. Yet we respond, at times at the risk of our own well being. Governments answer with aid, organizations with money, people with donations of all kind, but it is the healthcare providers who will step off the boat or plane into a ruined world that just a few hours earlier was a thriving and happy community. There, standing ankle deep in flood and blood, looking into the anxious eyes of young and old, applying bandages, suturing wounds, stabilizing fractures and administering the needed medication.

In the past we were often alone or in small groups with no backup or support. When I was in Dominica, I couldn't even call my own family to report my status. So getting qualified help was non-existent. Today however we are much luckier. Technology has put instruments at our disposal that allows us to contact professional help from large centers thousands of miles away. New communication tools allow experts to literally look over our shoulders from afar and guide our eyes and hands. The same technology has also made it possible to alert citizens of coming catastrophes, and to get them prepared and to shelters. In 1991, when Cyclone 02B hit Bangladesh, it killed 139,000 people. In comparison, Mora killed only six.

Our world is changing. Although political and climate changes present us with ever new challenges, our technology could keep us ahead of the oncoming calamities. But only if we have the wisdom to utilize it properly.

THE ECLIPSE

On Aug. 21, 2017, I, like millions of others, was twisting and stretching my neck and head skyward watching the dance of the sun and the moon as they peekabooed across the sky. At the moment when the darkness of the moon overcame the all powerful face of the sun, awestruck I watched the reaction of nature around me, and saw how this momentary show of the universe had a profound affect on everything around us. I was reminded of the famous naturalist; John Muir's reflection: "When we try to pick out anything by itself, we find that it is bound fast by a thousand invisible cords that cannot be broken, to everything in the universe."

Lost in our human arrogance, we often forget how much a part of the universe we all are. How we are attached and connected to one another and all that is around us. How everything that we do affects every fiber of all that surrounds us. But perhaps the most profound are the calamities and tragedies people bring upon each other through wars, neglect, protectionism, etc. Let's not forget though, that mankind is of one family and what affects one of us affects all of us.

As healthcare providers we often see the effects of the actions of our fellowmen firsthand. But we are more fortunate than most others. We have at our disposal means and tools to make a difference for ourselves as well as others. We can bring positive and constructive change to many who need it, close and afar. For just as the actions of the sun and the moon thousands of miles away in the universe can turn a day into night, our benevolence too can turn someone's life around – even miles away.

WOODSTOCK

In August of 1969, I was in the United States Air force, stationed in Lakenheath, England. The phenomenon that came to be known as "Woodstock" was televised there as well as here in the U.S. How different groups of people related to it was fascinating and eye opening. One great thing about being in the military is that at any given time, one is surrounded by many with diverging opinions. And being in the medical corp./field, we are encircled by a varied array of educated and learned people as well as the average folk from all walks of life having been pulled into the military by the draft. So one could hear all kinds of comments about an event.

I was in my mid twenties and of the generation that put together and attended the affair. We, like those at Woodstock were captivated by the music, the solidarity, camaraderie and the message of peace and harmony in the world.

Those in their thirties and forties seemed gripped by what the future would/ could be bringing and our older comrades worried about how the past was changing. With everyone expressing their point of view, one could be spinning in the merry-go-round of thoughts. On top of that, we were showered by the many opinions of our British and European friends. While our singers, songwriters and bands were singing their message, the Beatles were causing their own sensation and proclaiming their ideology in their songs to the world. It was a changing time of history for sure.

Caring for the health of the many wounded in wars, sickened by the calamities brought to them by conflicts around the world and suffering due to the lack of attention they were receiving, brought with it, its own quagmire of thought provoking philosophies and dogma.

Today we are facing challenges of unprecedented conundrums. One wonders whether it is due to or despite the happenings of fifty years ago. All we know for sure is that societies seem to be in a tailspin and unless we wise up and find a middle ground of understanding and take control of our destiny, we could be heading for a crash. One that we may find difficult to recover from easily.

Healthcare providers are one group of people who see the catastrophic problems surrounding us first hand. We need to be vocal and take charge in pointing out what's coming our way.

SURVIVING THE STORM

It was amazing to see the day last so long. As we flew westward the sun seem to just hang on the horizon. Massive clouds below us stretched their angry arms into the sky but we soared well out of their reach. The rays of the sun penetrating their convoluted crevasses were not as fortunate. Their changing colors of light fought the shadows through the cloud canyons in the stormy sky below us. Occasional openings in the clouds revealed the darkening earth below. Lights were coming on in the towns and hamlets foretelling the approaching night. I watched and wondered at the changing world around and below us.

I was returning from a medical conference. The theme of the conference was the new discoveries in antibiotics and the wonderful promises they made in fighting some of the more tenacious infections nature sends our way. Looking down, I thought of all those afflicted with them and the wonderful news my colleagues and I were bringing them from our conference. I was giddy with excitement and couldn't wait to return to work and tell my patients and coworkers the news. It was 1980 and the future looked bright. But as I watched the night overtake the diminishing light of the day, something deep within me was alarmed by the fight we were waging against nature.

Today healthcare seems to be trapped in a storm of its own. There are those of us who soar above it all and others caught in its turbulence. Problems with antibiotics, opioids and other drugs being just some of the issues. The political maelstrom seems to be overlooking the very need for a healthcare system that should be helping the sick and injured. But while the politicians, special groups and Wall Street biggies each work to serve their own interest, we the healthcare providers have our own job to do and it is much more difficult today than it has ever been. While dodging the up and down drafts of today's tempest, we still need to help those who come to us for assistance. Fortunately for us, new communication tools give us a hand in navigating this storm. It is the tool we can use that not only will help us survive the gale but come out ahead no matter which way the final wind blows.

Practicing from the Heart

THREE

CULTURAL CONNECTIONS

One of my favorite drawings of M.C. Escher reveals a two dimensional repeating pattern of interlocking reptiles. From the lower part of the picture, one of the creatures detaches itself from the flat world of the paper and creeps upward into the three-dimensional world of the table, and climbs on to one of the artist's tools on the table - triumphant.

Escher was an artist and philosopher who marveled at the possibility of the duality of the world, and of life itself. He believed that there is an opposite to everything and every situation. That while one person may live in total chaos and gloom another can live in the same world and under the same situation and circumstances but totally content and happy.

The duality of our world often intertwines in ways that we cannot foresee or expect. In no profession is this more true than medicine for often we, the providers, are better off than those we treat. Into this "for profit" world of healthcare, many have come to capitalize. So it is that most people are caught in the ironic situation of being cared for by those who cannot fathom their predicament or understand it. These encounters can be scary and chaotic and become even more of a dilemma when the clash is between cultures. It is therefore imperative that we realize our position and communicate better with those under our care.

All throughout this book, I have talked about our Native American people of the Southwest, their culture and mores. I have first hand experience with them because New Mexico, where I have lived for the past fifty years, is Indian country and many of the people we treat are Native Americans. Not understanding their culture can result in misinterpretation of their needs and their miscomprehension of our intent.

One of the first things I learned when I began work with them was that their culture teaches them the value of tolerance and respect of others in ways different from ours. Especially if the *others* are elders, leaders, or professionals. One such value requires them to not interrupt others' speech and conversation. Often they wait to answer after you have finished talking to be assured that you *are* finished. It also facilitates their understanding of what was said. This pause is confusing to many of our fast talking, rushed providers and is often perceived as lack of communication or disagreement.

They also value our conversation as significant enough to see no reason to acknowledge or recognize it by thanking us. Frequently after we are done, they just leave without saying anything. This too confuses many of us and we perceive it as a sign of dissatisfaction. Yet it usually is far from the case. Hence it behooves us to learn and follow the ways of our patients.

A great surgeon I have had the privilege of working with was George Harrington. A pediatric orthopaedic surgeon who is a retired army veteran and joined our practice in Albuquerque for a few years before moving to Las Cruces, NM, where he practices now. Dr. Harrington is a tall, towering gentleman of Comanche race. His upbringing gives him a special perspective that is very helpful in treating children with special needs. He is uniquely qualified to deal with challenging pediatric orthopaedic problems. Although Albuquerque is home to Carrie Tingly Hospital - one of the top Pediatric Orthopaedic Hospitals in the country, Dr. Harrington's expertise stood out.

On one occasion, we were caring for a young man of about fourteen with Blount's Disease that gave him uneven leg lengths. This type of problem often requires multiple surgical procedures to straighten and lengthen the shorter leg. Joseph (not his real name), was a big African-American young man who, like all teens of his age, wanted to play sports and be with his friends. His severe tibia vara however prevented this and thus made him unhappy and indulged him to eat which added to his weight and in turn his problem. When he first came to us, he had a low opinion of doctors. He already had several operations of his leg and was not at all looking forward to more surgeries, casts, and immobilization. Dr. Harrington's calm, reassuring and professional attitude however, soothed Joseph's concerns and over the next few years that we cared for him, he continued his treatment with us but with the zeal of a person with a new view and positive prospects in life. I don't know that we did anything different in his surgical care than other doctors he had seen, but how we related to him and his family made an immense difference in his accepting of his fate.

Children are not the only ones who need help facing their tragedies. Many adults too often need our assistance. When I was in the Air Force, a military lawyer from the Judge Advocate office broke his leg while playing soccer. It was the beginning of the season and, understandably, he was upset. While I was putting a cast on his leg, I noticed that he was at the verge of crying and made a comment that "now I have to stand on the sidelines hiding my cast while watching the game."

He was leaning back on the gurney and not looking at me or my work. When I finished his cast, I built a replica of the 'scale of justice' out of plaster over his cast. Then I showed it to him and said; "Now you don't have to hide your cast."

His face changed from sadness to hilarious laughter.

Later, he returned grateful and wrote a letter to my commanding officer on how I changed a terrible time into a tolerable one for him, and thanked me for it.

When I served on the NM Medical Board, the most single common complaint of the patients was the way they were treated by their providers and how little communication there was between them. Communication is a two-way street and need not be complicated. A simple show of concern and patience in dealing with people is usually all it takes.

Making sure that we understand our patient's problem and convey our instruction to their satisfaction is the key. This does not require any degree of literary acumen, just a clear conveyance of information.

The PA School I attended was in the US Public Health Hospital in Staten Island, New York. It was during the Viet Nam war and a shortage of doctors necessitated hiring foreign trained physicians for public health jobs. The hospital was the key healthcare facility for merchant marine sailors from around the world who happened to get sick or injured while traveling through US waters. It was not unusual to have a foreign patient – who knew little English – be treated by a foreign doctor with equally limited knowledge of our language. Some of the interactions were truly comical and yet of concern since it had to do with the care of people. Still the care was very good and it was heartwarming to see the diligent effort of our foreign colleagues in dealing with the challenges. To this day, I remember a page from a patient's chart describing the history of an incident written by a Chinese physician. It went something like this; "Man sat on toilet. Wife come home not know man sat on toilet. Wife open door hit man in eye. Man have bump in eye. First small bump now big bump."

On first read, it may show poor English and vocabulary. But it clearly and distinctly describes the incident. Shakespeare couldn't describe it better!

As I have emphasized at the start of this book, no matter what our profession, we all strive to be the best and achieve stardom in our work. Just like the lizard in Escher's drawing, crawling out of the flat picture, climbing over books and objects in it's table top world to the highest point it could reach to send a snort of smoke in satisfaction and triumph. To quote Escher himself; "Reaching the pinnacle of its existence. Yet after its victory, it finds itself returning to its flat, static, home on the paper to close the circle of life." So it is for us that no matter how successful we are in life and what pinnacles we reach, it is how we communicate with others that will determine how we are remembered even long after we are gone.

SEPTEMBER

Of Note in September

September 2, 1789 – The U.S. Treasury was created by Congress.

September 2, 1945 – Ho Chi Minh proclaimed the independence of Democratic Republic of Vietnam.

September 2, 1963 – Alabama Governor George Wallace forcibly halted public school integration by encircling Tuskegee High School with state troopers.

September 4, 1609 – The island of Manhattan was discovered by navigator Henry Hudson.

September 4, 1781 – El Pueblo de la Reina de Los Angeles (The Town of the Queen of the Angels) was founded by the Spanish Governor of California, Felipe de Neve. Later it was changed to Los Angeles.

September 4, 1957 – Arkansas governor Orval Faubus ordered the National Guard to bar nine black students from entering Central High School in Little Rock. In response, President Dwight D. Eisenhower sent in the 101st Airborne Division to make sure the students could enroll. Eisenhower in a televised speech to the nation said, "Mob rule cannot be allowed to override the decisions of our courts."

September 5, 1774 – The First Continental Congress assembled in Philadelphia with 56 delegates, representing every colony, except Georgia.

September 5, 1997 – Mother Teresa died in Calcutta at age 87. She spent her life aiding the sick and poor in India through her Missionaries of Charity order.

September 6, 1860 (1935) – American social worker; Jane Addams was born in Cedarville, Illinois. In 1883, she toured many European cities and was deeply moved by the hunger and misery she saw there. On her return, she founded Hull House in Chicago to serve the sick and poor and ran it for 46 years.

September 9, 1776 – The Continental Congress changed the name of the United Colonies to the United States.

September 11, 2001 – The worst terrorist attack in U.S. history occurred as four large passenger jets were hijacked and flown into buildings in NY and Washington, DC, killing nearly 3,000 people.

September 13, 1788 – The U.S. Congress chose New York as the capital of the new American government.

September 13, 1814 – Francis Scott Key watched the Battle of Fort Henry in Baltimore Harbor from a ship and was touched to see the American flag still flying over the fort at dawn. Inspiring him to write the verses, which in 1931, becomes the U.S. National Anthem.

September 13, 1851 (1902) – Dr. Walter Reed was born in Gloucester County, Virginia. He served as an army surgeon for more than 20 years and is known for his Yellow Fever research. The U.S. Army's general hospital in Washington, D.C., is named in his honor.

September 14, 1960 – The Organization of Petroleum Exporting Countries (OPEC) was formed by representatives of oil–producing countries meeting in Baghdad.

September 16, 1620 – *Mayflower* departed from England, bound for America with 102 passengers and crew, reaching Provincetown, Massachusetts on November 21st.

September 16, 1810 – Mexico broke from Spain as Father Miguel Hidalgo y Costilla rang the church bells in town of Dolores Hidalgo and encouraged the local Indians to "recover from the hated Spaniards the land stolen from your forefathers..."

September 16, 1908 – General Motors was founded by entrepreneur William Crapo "Billy" Durant in Flint, Michigan.

September 16, 1982 – A twoday massacre of Palestinian refugees began as Christian militiamen (the Phalangists) entered Sabra and Shatila camps in West Beirut and began shooting hundreds of Palestinian elderly men, women and children.

September 17, 1862 – The bloodiest day in U.S. military history occurred as the Confederate armies were confronted at Antietam in Maryland by the superior Union forces. By nightfall 26,000 men were dead, wounded, or missing.

September 19, 1893 – New Zealand became the first country to grant women the right to vote.

September 22, 1791 (1867) – British scientist Michael Faraday was born in Surrey, England. His discovery of electromagnetic induction resulted in the development of electric generators.

September 22, 1996 – Australian Bob Dent, a cancer victim, became the first person to commit legally assisted suicide by a lethal injection.

September 23rd – Autumn begins in the Northern Hemisphere. In the Southern Hemisphere today is the beginning of spring.

September 27, 1840 (1902) – American political cartoonist Thomas Nast was born in Landau, Germany. He created the symbols of the Democratic donkey and the Republican elephant.

September 29, 1789 – Congress created the United States Army.

September 29, 1901 (1954) – Enrico Fermi was born in Rome. He was a Nuclear physicist that developed a method of nuclear fission, which led to the development of the Atomic bomb.

VOLUNTEERS

Among the stack of mail was a card from The Salvation Army thanking me for a donation I had made earlier. It gave me time to pause. What an easy way to feel gratified; put a check in an envelope, mail it and go on about your business. Your money would – supposedly – help those in need. But is it really that easy. Do we really feel satisfied? Could we do more? It was interesting that the above card arrived on August 26, on the birthday of a young girl born in 1910 in Skopje, Albania (today's Macedonia). Her name was Anjeze Gonxhe Bojaxhiu. Her father died when she was eight and the family's poor status worsened. Her strong mother's faith however, helped the family cope and developed a sense of obligation and devotion in the young Gonxhe. So much so that at the age of eighteen she left home and joined the Sisters of Loreto at Loreto Abbey in Rathfarnham, Ireland. There she learned English, geography, catechism, and history. In 1931, at the age of twenty, she took her first religious vows as a nun. Soon after she was sent to Calcutta, India to serve at a convent there.

In Calcutta, the terrible poverty around her disturbed her so much that she felt compelled to leave the sanctuary of the convent and live among the poor. She exchanged her traditional habit for a simple white cotton sari with a blue border that became her signature garment for the rest of her life. Although she had no income and had to beg for food and supplies, she persevered, and soon after, the Vatican recognized her work and helped her start a congregation there. She gave her services wholeheartedly to the poorest of the poor and came to be recognized by much of humanity. So that by the time of her death in 1997, her relentless devotion to serving the poor had gotten the attention of the world and her Missionaries of Charity grew to be an international institution in 133 countries. She opened orphanages, homes for people with tuberculosis and leprosy, health clinics, and schools. She even opened shelters in Harlem and Greenwich Village in the United States.

She was awarded the Nobel Peace Prize in 1979. When asked how she found time to do all her charity work, she said, "I work all day. That is the only way. By blood, I am an Albanian. By citizenship, I am Indian. By faith, I am a Catholic nun. As to my calling, I belong to the world. As to my heart, I belong entirely to the Heart of Jesus."

When she was at the convent in Ireland she changed her name after Thérèse de Lisieux, the patron saint of missionaries but opted for the Spanish spelling of Teresa. We know her better as "Mother Teresa."

Remembering that it was her birthday and all that she had done for our world, I felt shame for feeling satisfaction in sending a check to The Salvation Army. We can do so much better.

THE UNIQUE SEED OF HUMAN CREATION

A great thing about America's Southwest is the diversity of its people. The Navajo Nation with over 300,000 population encompasses more than 27,000 square miles of the states of Arizona, New Mexico and Utah. Along with several other tribes and pueblos, they have a dominating presence making this area truly Indian Country. Many of us in healthcare deal with this wonderful group of people on a daily basis. My personal experiences with them have been very rewarding and enlightening. Over the years I have learned much and developed a high regard and respect for their way and philosophy of life. It is fascinating how similar their beliefs are to many old world cultures and customs.

A while back, I was visiting a colleague who is a Native American on the Navajo reservation and she asked if I could go with her to see her aunt who had injured her leg. She told me that her aunt had not been off the reservation for many years. "She lost her husband a while back and had been living by herself, isolated and happy. Local people and the Navajo Police check on her once in a while and bring her provisions in exchange for one of her sheep or goats. She does just fine without electricity and indoor plumbing. Computers, internet and even cell phones are completely alien to her."

Her aunt lived about thirty miles deeper into the reservation. We drove her 4WD off the pavement about 3 miles past her house and headed into the high country of the Navajo world on a dirt road. About twenty miles down that road, we turned off on to a primitive road and headed deeper into the hills. Finally we reached her aunt's house at the end of what was now more like a trail than a road. She lived in a one-room adobe dwelling with no electricity or running water.

Her leg was swollen and discolored but she was still walking on it with the help of a self-made cane. Even through the edema, I could feel the incongruity of the bone. "There is an obvious fracture here," I told my friend. "I think we should take her back with us and get an x-ray of her leg." She smiled and told me that she will not come with us but still translated. To make a long story short, all our reasoning and rationalizing was for naught. She had a herd of sheep and goats to care for and would not leave them. Despite the fact that we promised to return her home the same day. I started to insist but my friend stopped me and said; "You are not listening to her, she won't go!"

There were good pulses and sensory and motor functions were intact. So we applied the leg brace my friend had so thoughtfully brought with her and showed her how to apply it properly. She patiently listened and even practiced it a couple of times. Then carefully folded the brace and set it aside.

Once we were done with our exam and stopped our fussing over her as a patient, she began being a motherly host and insisted on feeding us before we left. It seemed to be more of an importance to her than our house call. So much so that I was overwhelmed by her kindness and true pleasure in having us there that I embraced her with a hug. How she totally relaxed into my arms surprised me and for that moment I experienced the warmth and soul of being an Indian.

On the way back, my friend and I exchanged stories. I told her of my family, my grandmother, our traditions and she told me of hers. We marveled at the connection and cultural similarity of our people, of all people. *The unique seed of human creation* and how if we were to take away our negative prejudicial teachings, we would all live in blessed harmony. Still, we felt a gratitude that those like her aunt keep traditions alive and are the foundation of our old cultures.

Today telehealth and telemedicine can help provide for our Native Americans living in such isolation while preserving their culture and way of life. Understanding cultures and respecting their lifestyle allows us to be respected by them, thus developing a mutual appreciation, which in turn will help in trusting each other. The technology of telehealth makes it possible to enter their world without interfering with it. We must assure however that in using it we don't lose our humanity.

NOT SO EASY TASKS

In 2018, due to an increase in our international readership, we had to transition our website (TH Pulse - The Healthcare Pulse) to a new hosting company. What seemed to be a simple conversion became a daunting task which gave us a fresh appreciation of what technical people go through on a daily basis. When we first started our website, back in the 1990s, all we had to be concerned with was getting the HTML codes right. Today, not only do the codes have to be correct, the site has to be secured, and has to be accessible by multiple devices, on multiple platforms and operating systems. Our initial belief was that it all gets done automatically – well yes and no. We thought that all we had to do was to write the content and the process would take care of itself – well no, not exactly. So none of what we considered to be straight forward was. An eye opener for this old timer. At times, I felt totally lost.

I was reminded of the time a neighbor's backhoe developed a leak in the hydraulics. We lived way up in the northern part of the state with no technical expertise available except that of our neighbors. And if there was one thing *they* were all good at, it was being expert in all things they knew nothing about. After all, all they had to do was disconnect the doohickey from the whatchamacallit and replace it with a new one, right? Wrong.

The annoying leaking hose was disconnected and the neighbor took it to the dealer in the big city - nearly two hundred miles away and came back with a new one and a whole lot of instructions mostly on what *NOT* to do. The next day half dozen heads came together and started screwing and connecting and pumping and filling and whatever else seemed appropriate. I came home just in time to see the finale and watched in amazement as they all stood back proudly while our neighbor started the confounded machine and with the first flexion of the arm, snapped the brand-new hose in half. Pressurized oil and curses went flying all over the countryside. And well you can guess the rest of the story.

Today with the Internet, YouTube, Google and thousands of other advisers, things should be easier. All we have to say is thank God for the young people at the support centers of all these companies whose sales people promise that you can do – whatever you are trying to do – in under one hour.

In medicine too, we all had to deal with patients who came to us with advice from neighbors, relatives, etc. on how they should be treated and wanting to know why we are not listening to those sage recommendations. Which brings us to the concept of telehealth and telemedicine. Though expert counsel and guidance are available, many false ones float around the ocean of the Internet as well. So it behooves us to be weary of what we say and whom we say it to. Building a reliable platform for use by colleagues near and far is a lot more complicated than commonly perceived and expected. Best recommendation is to let the real experts do the consulting – those in university settings or major healthcare institutions. We hope readers are guided to the true authorities and professionals.

WHERE FORTUNE ROAMS

In the far west corner of Texas, in the city of El Paso, the campus of the University of Texas, El Paso (UTEP) adorns the bleak face of the surrounding hills and town. Built in Bhutanese Architecture, it invites all imagination to a profoundly spiritual state. As though the very notion of edification will bring one closer to God. Inspiring one to reach for that desirous unknown as an acolyte would, worshipping his promising deity.

Less than half a mile to the south, seen from the dusty and famine blown shanty houses of Juarez, Mexico, UTEP beckons onlookers proudly and invitingly. A clear picture of richness, fortune and progress. One can imagine a young teenager looking across the river, fence and highway at the picture in front, wondering and asking; "*Why?*" For such fortune and opportunity are completely unavailable to him or her – yet so close.

What do you tell a child full of life, when teacher, parent and Bible tells him that bettering himself is reaching for paradise. Yet his reaching gaze and outstretched arms find only the madness of mankind and barriers in front. For whether looking across Rio Grande, Mediterranean, jungle, or Sahara the unreachable indicates an empty and hopeless life ahead.

The United Nations Census tells us that people under 25 make up 43 percent of the world's population, and 60 percent of the population of developing countries. That is more than 3 billion people and a lot of restless energy. Consider that among them are a few of the like of Mozart, Einstein and Galileo. Perhaps even a few Hitlers, Pol Pots, or Idi Amins. So wouldn't we want to encourage the former and control the latter?

Yet disparities abound in our world as inequalities are often caused by the very people who close their borders. Discriminations have sparked discontent into raging fires of revolution and chaos. With every revolt, more people are displaced, become refugees and homeless. The increase of such masses closes more borders, fences are strengthened and walls are erected. People are made lost and desperate, adding to the instability.

Such conditions sicken men, women and children – mentally as well as physically. So to us (providers) they come for help. For us, such disparities create a dilemma to which we are strained to find an answer. For, with our Hippocratic oath, we have promised "… to abstain from all intentional wrong-doing and harm, especially from abusing the bodies of man or woman, bond or free. …" Yet we too often find ourselves behind the same barriers.

The world's defense spending is about 1.7 trillion dollars. Just one percent of that could educate every child in the world. Our new technology can help us provide medical and educational help to everyone on both sides of the disparate and dispirited world. Fortunately new communication tools allow us to traverse rivers, walk through fences and climb over the walls of misfortune! We only need the courage to set aside our own prejudices and use it to help each other. Then maybe that half a mile won't seem so far after all.

CITIZENSHIP DAY

September 17 is Citizenship day. With the movement of all the migrants, refugees, and seekers of a better life, the world is being literarily remade and the ramification of all the changes is profound and will be long lasting. Politics aside, we all have to appreciate the fact that seeking a better life is a fundamental and natural desire that all creatures of God have and strive for. Although our birthplace may determine our race and certain minor anatomical differences, it should not bind us to a permanent geographical region. After all, if not for man's desire to migrate, explore and search of betterment, we all would still be living in Africa.

We should remember that much of the scientific, technological, and medical advancement – we are so proud of – was brought here or invented by immigrants. There is an old saying that; "Every man is born twice. First to the parents and family that bore him and second to the people and society he/she chooses to live with." We the people of this planet must share its resources equally and evenly. Only then, man's true potential for advancement and achievement will propel him forward to new accomplishments. Let us share this passion of being human with all mankind and truly move ourselves into the Twenty First Century and beyond. Let us use our technology to the betterment of all people, for after all, we are all citizens of this small planet.

THE INTERNATIONAL DAY OF PEACE

September 21 is The International Day of Peace. Established in 1981 by the United Nations General Assembly as a day devoted to strengthening the ideals of peace, both within and among all nations and peoples. In 2015 The United Nations Member States adopted the 17 Sustainable Development Goals because they understood that it would not be possible to build a peaceful world if steps were not taken to achieve economic and social development for all people everywhere and ensure that their rights were protected.

Nothing in the world could be more peaceful than a healthy community, and nothing could show more peaceful intentions than caring for your foe's mental and physical well-being. New technology makes it possible to care for your friends and foes by providing them the necessary means and advice without endangering any of your own people. Sharing medical knowledge to improve your enemy's health is a gift that cannot be ignored or underestimated. Such acts of kindness and good intentions surely reveal benevolence and work toward true peace.

As stated by the UN Secretary-General António Guterres: "It is time all nations and all people live up to the words of The Universal Declaration of Human Rights, which recognizes the inherent dignity and equal and inalienable rights of all members of the human race. ..."

We must share our planet's resources to the benefit of all. Only then man's true potential for advancement and achievement will propel him forward to new accomplishments. Only then can we truly become A *family of man* and live in peace.

MEMORY

Seat 4A placed me by the window on my way back from Florida. The early flight was half full and as we flew west, I watched the rivalry between day and night in the country below. Almost all my fellow travelers were sleeping. I was glued to the window, watching the lights of the towns flickering and going out with the arriving day. I recall thinking, "They have all heard of Elvis and know who the Beatles are. But I wonder how many know the name of their doctor?" Mementos of sand and sea safely stored in the archives of my mind, I reflected on the gift of memory.

When my children were in high school, I drove them to school every morning. Occasionally, another student would carpool with us. Once, an exchange student from Scandinavia was with us - a junior who was staying with a neighbor of ours. She was a charming young lady who spoke with a strong accent. The radio was on the morning show and played a variety of songs. The next song caught her attention and she announced; "Oh, Louie Armstrong."

I was surprised that she knew the jazz master and asked if he was popular in Sweden. "Oh yes, my father owns many of his albums. He often plays a song or two on the radio when *he* takes us to school in the morning. This song makes me homesick."

It is a strange thing; memory! How simple things in passing can awaken deep emotions or echoes of past events. There are things that we will remember forever and then those that are erased as dust by the passing wind. The fact that we have the ability to file them in our long term or short term memories is not in itself surprising. But what we choose to store, is.

Why so many of us recall such menial things as certain musicians, bands, actors or characters, yet cannot remember who the governor of our state or our senator is, or our doctor's instruction regarding diet and exercise. In remembering selectively, do we make our lives better or just easier to cope with? I suppose the tsunami of irrelevant daily data bombarding us makes this selective remembrance a necessity.

As practitioners we face this dilemma daily. How do we make our patients follow our instructions and not forget them as soon as they get into their car and turn the radio on? Perhaps having the ability to remind our patients of our instructions would be beneficial. My dentist routinely calls his patients in the evening after their visit to check on them and remind them of his instructions – a wonderful idea.

Fortunately today's technology provides us this ability. Tele-education and telehealth are two instruments in our medical-bag that we can use. But we must first care enough for our patients to make this extra effort. The hectic life we ourselves live however, make this ever more challenging and the organizations we work for often make such efforts prohibitive. If we want to make lasting impression on our patients though, it behooves us to remind them of us and our concern for them. Otherwise the memory of their visit will be erased as footsteps in the sand by the passing wave.

WHEN DISASTER AFFECTS MORE THAN THE DISASTER AREA

It is always heart breaking when disaster strikes a part of our nation or the world. But the string of calamities that have been affecting our world in the past few years are definitely testing the limits of our ability to cope. Even a wealthy and powerful country such as ours feels the tremendous weight of such tragedies. More importantly though, are the far reaching effects of these events. For while everyone focuses on the center of destruction, damages to outlying infrastructures and businesses are often more long lasting and expensive and affect places far from the disaster centers.

The healthcare industry is perhaps more affected than others. Not only by having to provide care to the needy but often in ways not envisioned. Case in point is the interruption of drug manufacturing in Puerto Rico by a hurricane that could cause shortages in far away places. Or the destruction of medical school infrastructures on many Caribbean Islands housing them, disturbing their students' education. Or damage done to many rural hospitals and nursing homes around Houston, having to transfer their patients to places as far away as Dallas, San Antonio, and New Orleans. The recent pandemic isolating many and restricting travel affects international commerce as well as passengers. That includes getting medical help, supplies, medications, and vaccines to many needy areas. Especially the rural and hard to reach communities. It is surprising that many dreaded diseases find their way to such isolated places, but medical help finds it hard to reach them.

Disease aside, the unpredictable disasters such as the earthquakes in Mexico, Japan, Volcanoes in Hawaii, Iceland, and Italy are example of healthcare need. Besides all the damage that was done to buildings, burying hundreds of people in their ruble, many small businesses were totally destroyed, forever ruining the livelihood of families. The global natural changes are here to stay for the foreseeable future. How do we prepare to deal with them is the question.

Despite all these horrendous tragedies, today's technology provides us with plenty of tools to help our fellow human beings. It can help those on the frontlines get help from the experts in centers far away. Find vacancies for patients and make available their medical records – no matter where they end up.

New communication tools can supervise the first responders to provide the best care possible. It can help transfer the production of drugs from damaged plants to other pharmaceutical manufacturing centers through transmission of the drug formula, 3D printing and other controls. Tele-education can continue teaching the medical students – wherever they are – while their school arranges for restructuring. Small businesses can receive government oversight and financial support while they plan their future.

Maybe our world *is* facing more challenges but upon closer examination, we find that the solutions are also at hand. When the United Nations General Assembly meets annually in New York, many leaders of the world present the challenges they are facing. But there is one clear thing present, the hope that their problems can be resolved. No one has lost hope in resolving their problems but ask that the rest of us be aware of their needs and help them work it out. No one is planning for failure but the world is worried that we are failing to plan properly. The world needs to channel resources toward the constructive efforts needed to address these issues. We can help!

MARCO POLO

Sept 23, 1215 was the birthday of Kublai Khan, the Chinese ruler whose empire stretched across modern day China and Mongolia. He founded the Yuan Dynasty. He is also known to be the first to institute paper money.

Despite his popularity and tremendous achievements, he would have been unknown to us, were it not for the writings of Marco Polo who visited China during this time. It took Marco Polo three years to travel there. He was a teenager when he started the journey with his father and uncle. He spent seventeen years in China and another three years to return to Europe.

Marco Polo praised Kublai as a great leader but gave conflicting reports on the emperor's life in his writings. Considering his seventeen years of experience there, it is understandable to see how witnessing the running of such an empire could leave varying impressions on a young mind.

One of the emperor's excesses that impressed Marco Polo was his summer palace. The place was called Shang-tu, a word that became known as Xanadu in English. Shang-tu however just meant "Upper Capital," distinguishing it from the main capital he founded to the south. The place had mystical powers and was the subject of many writings by Marco Polo, Samuel Coleridge and others. Today, Kublai's main establishment is known as Beijing and all that remains of Shang-tu is several hills on a vast plain.

Interesting how empires change, rulers die, palaces become ruins and history paints diverging pictures of events. It is also fascinating to note that the entire human history occurred in a tiny period of geological time on this small planet of ours. Marco Polo's adventures took twenty-three years of his life. Today we can traverse the same distance that took Polo three years, in a few short hours. Write about it, publish it and send it to millions of readers by Internet. These technological advances have made us aware of how small our planet really is.

Just before the *Voyager 1* spacecraft left our solar system in 1990, Carl Sagan convinced NASA to turn it around and take a last family picture of our solar system. The picture showed earth as a blue dot in the darkness of the universe. Later, at a lecture, Sagan reflected that "On that dot, every human being who ever lived, whether prince or pauper, rich or poor, smart or simple lived out their lives."

The picture clearly reveals how small we really are, yet our ego and our audacity made taking that picture possible. Though many credit a few scientists for making that picture possible, were it not for humanity as a whole, the existence of those few would not have happened. So we owe our achievements to the entire human race and should not take our humanity for granted nor subject it to peculiar prejudices. As Alexis Tsipras, the Greek Prime Minister in his address to the UN General Assembly in September 2016 elegantly stated; "Humanity should not be conditional."

Many challenges face us all on this blue dot today. Not the least is the challenge of healthcare for our people. Fortunately, the same technology that made taking the selfie of earth from four billion miles away possible, gives us the ability to see and care for each other right here on earth. We just need the wherewithal to use it. How would Marco Polo write about it today, I wonder?

OCTOBER

Of Note in October:

October 1, 1908 – Henry Ford's Model T went on sale for the first time.

October 1, 1949 – The People's Republic of China was founded with Mao Zedong as Chairman.

October 1, 1979 – After 70 years of American control, the Panama Canal Zone was formally handed over to Panama.

October 2, 1869 (1948) – Mohandas (Mahatma) Gandhi was born in Porbandar, India. He is known for his devout lifestyle and nonviolent resistance, which ended British rule over India. He was assassinated on January 30, 1948.

October 2, 1871 (1955) – Cordell Hull was born in Pickett County, Tennessee. He served in both houses of Congress, as Secretary of State, and was instrumental in the establishment of the United Nations.

October 2, 1908 (1993) – Thurgood Marshall was sworn in as the first African-American associate justice of the U.S. Supreme Court.

October 3, 1863 – President Abraham Lincoln issued a proclamation designating the last Thursday in November as Thanksgiving Day.

October 3, 1932 – Iraq gained independence from Britain and joined the League of Nations.

October 4, 1582 – The Gregorian Calendar was adopted in Catholic countries.

October 4, 1957 – The Space Age began as the Russians launched the first satellite; Sputnik I into orbit.

October 5, 1882 (1945) – Robert Goddard was born in Worcester, Massachusetts. He is considered to be the Father of the Space Age.

October 5, 1986 – U.S. Marine Eugene Hasenfus was captured by Nicaraguan Sandinistas after a plane carrying arms for the Nicaraguan rebels (Contras) was shot down over Nicaragua. The beginning of the "Iran-Contra" controversy in the Reagan White House after it was revealed that money from the sale of arms to Iran was used to fund covert operations in Nicaragua.

October 6, 1846 (1914) – Engineer and inventor George Westinghouse was born in Central Bridge, New York. He developed air brakes for trains and adopted alternating current (AC) systems for electric power transmission in the U.S.

October 10, 1813 (1901) – Italian opera composer; Giuseppi Verdi was born in Le Roncole, Italy. His operas are among the most popular today.

October 10, 2014 – At age 17, Malala Yousafzai from Pakistan became the youngest Nobel Peace Prize winner.

October 11, 1939 – Albert Einstein suggested to President Franklin D. Roosevelt that the U.S. develop the atomic bomb. It resulted the "Manhattan Project."

October 11, 1962 – The Second Vatican Council was opened in St. Peter's Basilica in Rome by Pope John XXIII. It resulted in changes to the Catholic Church including the use of English and local native languages in the Mass instead of Latin, and cooperation with other religions and denominations.

October 12, 1492 – Christopher Columbus made landfall in the New World in the Bahamas.

October 12, 1811 – Paraguay declared its independence from Spain and Argentina.

October 12, 1822 – Brazil became independent of Portugal.

October 13, 1775 – The United States Navy was created by the Second Continental Congress.

October 13, 1884 – Greenwich was established as the universal time from which standard times throughout the world are calculated.

October 14, 1644 (1718) – William Penn was born in London. In 1681, he received a Royal charter with a large land grant in America from King Charles II. The land grant later became the State of Pennsylvania.

October 14, 1947 – U.S. Air Force Captain Chuck Yeager broke the sound barrier.

October 14, 1964 – Civil Rights leader Martin Luther King, Jr., received the Nobel Peace Prize. He donated the $54,000 in prize money to the Civil Rights movement.

October 15, 1844 (1900) – German philosopher Friedrich Nietzsche was born in the Province of Saxony.

October 16, 1701 – Yale University was founded in Killingworth, Connecticut and later moved to New Haven in 1716.

October 16, 1758 (1843) – Noah Webster was born in West Hartford, Connecticut. He compiled the first American dictionary.

October 16, 1854 (1900) – Oscar Wilde was born in Dublin, Ireland.

October 16, 1964 – China detonated its first nuclear bomb at the Lop Nor test site in Sinkiang.

October 16, 1995 – The Million Man March took place in Washington, D.C., under the direction of Nation of Islam leader Louis Farrakhan, who delivered the main address to the gathering of African-Americans.

October 19, 1960 – The U.S. embargo of Cuba began.

October 20, 1818 – The 49th parallel was set as the U.S. Canadian border.

October 22, 1811 (1886) – Hungarian composer Franz Liszt was born in Raiding, Hungary.

October 24, 1945 – The United Nations was founded.

October 25, 1881 (1973) – Pablo Picasso was born in Malaga, Spain.

October 25-30, 1983 – The Caribbean island of Grenada was invaded by 2,000 US Marines and Army Rangers.

October 26, 1825 – The Erie Canal opened as the first major manmade waterway in America, linking Lake Erie with the Hudson River.

October 27, 1904 – The New York City subway opened.

October 28, 1636 – Harvard University, the oldest institution of higher learning in America, was founded in Cambridge, Massachusetts.

October 28, 1886 – The Statue of Liberty was dedicated on Bedloe's Island in New York Harbor.

October 28, 1914 (1995) – Dr. Jonas Salk was born in New York City. In 1952, he developed the vaccine for Polio.

October 28, 1919 – Prohibition began in the U.S. It lasted nearly 14 years and became highly profitable for organized crime.

October 28, 1955 – Microsoft founder Bill Gates was born in Seattle, Washington. In 1975, he co-founded Microsoft with Paul Allen, designing software for IBM computers.

October 28, 1971 – The British House of Commons voted 356 – 244 in favor of joining the European Economic Community.

October 29, 1929 – The stock market crashed as over 16 million shares were dumped amid tumbling prices. The Great Depression followed in America, lasting until the outbreak of World War II.

October 31st is Halloween or All Hallow's Eve, an ancient celebration combining the Christian festival of All Saints with Pagan autumn festivals.

PEOPLE OF MEDICINE

Among the massive news of disasters, calamities, crimes and aggressions in Octobers of recent years, were tidbits of good news that should have been the focus of our attention. One such report, for example, was of the Nobel Prize in Medicine, awarded jointly to scientists, Jeffrey C. Hall, Michael Rosbash and Michael W. Young "For their discoveries of molecular mechanisms controlling the circadian rhythm" In 2017.

And awarded jointly to James P. Allison and Tasuku Honjo "for their discovery of cancer therapy by inhibition of negative immune regulation" in 2018.

And awarded jointly to William G. Kaelin Jr, Sir Peter J. Ratcliffe and Gregg L. Semenza "for their discoveries of how cells sense and adapt to oxygen availability" in 2019.

And awarded jointly to Harvey J. Alter, Michael Houghton and Charles M. Rice "for the discovery of Hepatitis C virus" in 2020. Our sincerest congratulations and best wishes to these outstanding researchers.

It is interesting that many Nobel Prizes these days are awarded jointly to several people. Often from different parts of the world. As we can see the prizes for medicine included, for medicine is a collaborative and cooperative science. Especially in today's advanced and complicated environment. Our scientists are attempting research in areas that a few years ago would not be achievable. This is a credit to the advanced technologies of our time. It must be remembered that our researchers have many supportive staff and assistants to help them accomplish their work. Much like a fine tuned orchestra conducting together, a research team also depends on each individual to perform his or her part perfectly. They too should be congratulated and saluted for their contribution. Especially when the work is shared by several schools, the number of supporters multiplies. The faculty and staff of these universities also need to be applauded.

The technology of telecommunication plays a major role in the work of our researchers and scientists today. In this respect, we have even more people to be thankful to. This type of supportive and shared work will help accomplish the new and wondrous discoveries for the betterment of mankind in the twenty first century. It is the cooperative work of the people of medicine that make life more challenging and interesting in a positive way in this troubled world. For in a way every one of us in healthcare is contributing to this work so it should be our responsibility to be aware of this achievement. We are not just treating someone's illness but contributing to the overall science that we are practicing. So we acknowledge and salute all of us. It is a pride we all share and a gratifying achievement to entice our students with – in all fields of medicine.

THE WORLD AND HEALTHCARE

In the fall, the United Nations General Assembly meets in New York. The state of the world, such as it is, demands better understanding and appreciation of these events. In the United Nations, as well as the United States, many are beating their chest to the drums of protectionism and patriotism.

All through the 2018, 2019 and 2020 assembly presentations at the UN, for example, we heard complaints and criticism about the injustices happening around the world. Whether it is the Rohingya, Syrians, Africans, Yemenis, Venezuelans or Central Americans, the refugee crisis is central to everyone's concern. Among the most alarming of complaints was the health status of these people. The world still remembers the influenza of 1918, the deadliest in history that killed an estimated 30 – 50 million. The present Covid-19 pandemic is another good example of this failure and how the denial of the scientific facts by several world leaders has added to the confusion and disorder of the chaos. It is disheartening that after a hundred years, not only have we not eliminated the cause of the world's core problems, we are contributing to them.

It was President Michel Temer of Federative Republic of Brazil who said it best: "… there is a piece of the world in every Brazilian." That could be said about every one of us in the Western Hemisphere. For unless one is from a native people, we are all immigrants or children of immigrants in this part of the world. We have come from Africa, Europe and Asia and brought a piece of it with us. It is this cultural fusion that makes the Western Hemisphere such a desirable destination. For, not only does it open for us a new part of the world, it shows that the mixture of cultures can produce a stronger and smarter civilization.

On a personal note, I can assert that my experience has been that whenever opportunity had me work with people of other cultures, the gained knowledge was greater and richer. I can tell many tales of such incidents. Here are two cases that portray the unparalleled level of such experiences:

Dr. Patel was a general surgeon from India whom I worked with on a Caribbean Island - he used to chant (under his breath) while operating. It created an immense atmosphere of peace in that room. Our anesthesiologist told me that on several occasions Dr. Patel's patients seem to be in a state of trance. Something he never saw when working with other surgeons.

In another meaningful experience, I was deployed to Jordan after the civil war as part of the American Red Cross. We joined other groups of the International Red Cross. There was a nurse with one of the European groups who was a nun. It was fascinating to watch the majority Muslim patients respect her to the point of reverence. They often said that she reminded them of Mary, mother of Jesus, and felt at peace in her presence. Although the prayers and religious beliefs of these providers seemed to play a role, I feel that it was their genuine concern and care for the patients that played the bigger part.

COLUMBUS DAY

Columbus day, a celebration of Americas founding is in October. It was in 1492 that the first immigrants arrived in the new world. The new world discovery became a source of riches and unlimited bounty for the explorers, their families, sires and countries.

Today the nearly eight billion inhabitants of the world are sweltering in some areas while basking in riches in others. It must be remembered that overcrowding and lack of adequate resources are the reason powerful nations have always overtaken the resources of others for their own use. But today many of these resources too are depleted. Thus the need for people to seek refuge elsewhere, only to face humiliating and genocidal consequences.

In the past few years, Nobel Peace Prizes have been awarded to activists and advocates of the victims of these injustices around the world. People like Martin Luther King, Mother Teresa, Nelson Mandela, Rigoberta Menchu Tum, Malala Yousafazi, Jane Addams and others. In 2018 the prize was awarded to two who have been on the forefront of these wars. Dr. Denis Mukwege, a Congolese physician who's been treating thousands of women who were victims of rape in Congo. And Nadia Murad, a Yazidi human rights activist and a victim herself of the wars in the Middle East.

It is interesting that 17 of the Nobel Peace Prize winners were women – more than any other category, ten of which were from the so-called developing countries and nine of which received their prize in the last 20 years. Two of the three youngest people to receive the Nobel Prize, received it in the Peace category. Listening to most of their speeches, the main concern they had was the health of the victims. The victims' fate and destiny lands them in such dire and inhumane conditions and sickness and disease follow them. While governments and international organizations struggle with their political and economical consequences, healthcare providers have to deal with their health issues on an individual and personal level. Often treating that which cannot be dealt with under such conditions. Perhaps if those objecting to these people's plight could only listen to the snuffled cries of children, smell the stench of wounds in a burn ward, or see the emaciated body of a starving individual with their own eyes, they would see the situation in a different light. Our Nobel Peace Prize recipients have seen these conditions first hand and tried to do something about them, only to pay for it with their lives or livelihood. Our world is crying, let's stop blaming and start helping. After all did not Columbus cross the ocean to find riches to replace the depleting resources of Europe?

BALLOON FIESTA

The first full week of October is the annual International Balloon Fiesta in Albuquerque, New Mexico. Hundreds of balloons from around the world gather and put on an unparalleled show. Hundreds of thousands of spectators too, come to watch the weeklong festivities.

I have been involved in our annual balloon fiesta activities since the beginning when it launched from the parking lot of a local mall. A good friend of mine; Jeff is a balloonist and had his balloon in the event and asked me to join him that day. We met about 5 AM in the parking lot. There were four of us, but soon a couple more trucks showed up. Jeff handed me a broom and pointed to an area behind his salvaged bread delivery truck. "We are going to spread the balloon canopy there, make sure there are no sharp objects or anything that can damage it.S"

In the early light of the day, I swept the ground as best I could and returned to the truck to help unload the balloon parts. Jeff connected the tanks to the burners and tested them. The canopy, called envelope, carefully unfolded and spread out. A powerful gas operated fan was placed at the opening. Several of us held the mouth open as Jeff started the fan and blew air into the envelope. It gyrated, rolled and began to inflate. Despite the early hours of the morning, several bystanders showed up, smiles exchanged, salutation made – balloon people are friendly folk, for one never knows whose help may be needed. We stood up taller and pretended to know what we were doing. Jeff turned the burners on, pointing it into the expanding envelope. The heat soon warmed the air inside and it started to rise. Jeff jumped in and instructed us to hold it down. Burners belching flames made the balloon struggle to break free from the ground. Myself and another passenger jumped into the basket as others let go of it and we left the earth and shot up into the cool air of the morning. We rose to meet the first rays of the sun, clearing the top of the Sandia Mountain. In the air, we were joined by several other balloons that had taken off from other locations around town. An exhilarating feeling overwhelmed me as a light wind got a hold of us and blew us across the landscape below. Sleepy Albuquerque slipped silently by under us. We looked shamelessly into many backyards while people slept. The occasional blast of the propane torch broke the silence and kept us aloft. Lost in the thrill of the moment, I looked at the world around me in silence.

The year was 1977 and we had just attended the fourth Albuquerque Balloon Fiesta. Years later, while working at Lovelace Medical Center, we established a First Aid and Medical Tent at the newly opened Balloon Fiesta Park. Communication was via walkie-talkies and was delayed. Whether we were piloting balloons and talking to our ground crew or receiving calls at the medical booth to alert us of injuries coming our way, connections were slow and often poor.

Most of what we cared for there were scrapes and scratches due to people falling or running into something while looking up at the many colorful balloons ascending into the blue skies of New Mexico. Among the thousands of visitors, there were occasional people who had forgotten their medicine. We checked them and refilled their medications. A few times, it became necessary to refer or shipped them to our ER. Occasionally, we tried – and usually failed – to contact the primary provider of the patient back in their hometown. The contact was established by a long distance phone call which often required us leaving a message and then waiting to hear back from them. If we did hear back, it usually was a day or two later and by then the patient had already left. Today, GPS, Internet, Cell Phones and the like make navigation, communication and information available instantly.

I have been involved with Telehealth and Telemedicine since its early years as well. Telehealth, Telemedicine, and Tele-education as well as ballooning have progressed considerably over the past few short years. Today people needing help and advice can reach healthcare institutions from every corner of the earth. Organizations such as American Telemedicine Association (ATA), UNM Project ECHO, Federation of State Medical Boards (FSMB) and The Addis Clinic in the US, along with others like the International Society for Telemedicine and eHealth (IsfTeH) in Switzerland and Swinfen Charitable Trust in UK are working very hard to improve access to Telehealth, Telemedicine, and Tele-education for everyone.

Our country and indeed the entire world are going through many changes – some good and some not. But we have always faced challenges and come through by uniting and confronting them. I recall a song from the 1950s by Bing Crosby called "Early American" in *You Can Change the World* that is worth listening to. If that is not enough, (as I have indicated earlier in this book) I recommend the book; *Did I ever tell you how Lucky You Are?* by the late Dr. Seuss. A book that I feel should be mandatory reading by all high school and college students.

Today, GPS, Internet, Cell Phones and the like make navigation, communication and information available instantly – in aviation as well as in the world of medicine. But accepting this new way of life is difficult for many of our people. Still change is here and technology is moving medicine – like aviation – forward. It behooves us to take charge of our destiny; otherwise others will do it for us at an unfavorable cost to us. It is better for medical professionals to control the advance of healthcare through technology, rather than technology adopting medicine to its needs. Let's work together to fully develop this system and make all our lives easier in this mobile society.

TABERNACLES
OF HEALTHCARE

Recently our world has witnessed many shocking disasters and calamities. The news media's dash to the scene along with the first responders shows the acute phase of such tragedies. The affected are rushed to the local medical centers and most of the time the news ends there. However for us healthcare providers, that is when the work begins, though seldom are we mentioned. It is also noteworthy to point out that disasters do not always have an acute phase to them. As a matter of fact some of the worst crises start slowly but due to lack of notice by the authorities and the media, do not receive attention till they become a full blown problem. Though these incidences may go unnoticed by the masses, our profession responds and cares for the deprived, often urgently, yet quietly and calmly.

A medical boat sails up the Amazon, a hospital ship docks in the Caribbean, a MASH unit moves close to the frontlines, the Red Cross prepares shelters for refugees, and the volunteer healthcare providers travel to affected areas – often at their own expense. We see and care for the needy first hand, frequently before any news media is alerted or governments take action.

It may surprise many that of the top ten countries with the highest fatalities from terrorism; four are in Central and South America. Today, the ever-increasing population and their migration – due to economics, crime, war or natural afflictions – create new challenges for us. It is understandable to respond to calamities brought upon us by wars, nature, famine, disease, and economic changes. But when the cause is an individual or group's demented ideology, anger or revenge, our work is even more heartbreaking. Still healthcare providers like us, rise to the occasion and confront these problems. By doing so, we provide the solace people seek when they come to our tabernacles of healthcare.

Healthcare providers have always been selflessly caring for the needy throughout history. At times in the most appalling environments such as during the epidemic of the Black Plague, numerous instances of Cholera and Yellow Fever outbreaks, and most recently the Covid-19 pandemic, Ebola, Zika and the many occurrences of viral respiratory diseases – see UN WHO's list of disease outbreaks by year on the UN website or search for it on Internet. So we acknowledge and salute our colleagues in all corners of the world. Keep up the good work and may God bless you all!

UNDERSTANDING EACH OTHER

Good communication is something I have been very concerned about in all my medical practice years. That is to make sure that we, practitioners and our patients, totally understand one another. For us, to understand what the patient's real problem is and our patients, to fully comprehend our diagnosis, prognosis and instructions we are giving them.

As I have mentioned numerous times the number one complain of patients about their providers is lack of proper communication. And when I sit on the NM Medical Review Commission hearings, the number one reason for lawsuits is misunderstandings between patients and providers. Nowhere is this more dangerous than when dealing with non- English speaking patients or an average patient who will not understand our medical jargon.

Our patient populations come from many national backgrounds and cultures. They bring with them their traditions, customs and rituals that most of us are unfamiliar with. Grasping their problems and needs is not always clear or simple. Consider this story told to me by a colleague who was a Vietnam veteran working in a local urgent care:

He was at work one day when he noticed a commotion across the clinic in another provider's section. There were shouts and angry exchanges so he went to investigate. There were police officers and others not from his clinic standing by.

"What is going on?" He asked a nurse.

"We called child protective services, because Doctor R. felt his young patient was abused. They are Vietnamese and don't speak English well."

It was early 1970s and the Vietnam War had just ended. Many Vietnamese were immigrating here. Since he had spent a couple of tours in Vietnam and knew a little of the language, he volunteered to intervene. Soon the problem became clear. The treating doctor of a young child had noticed several bruises on the child's body and had suspected abuse so he called the social services who called the child protective services, who called the police and they all ganged up on the poor family.

A Vietnamese folk remedy for many diseases is to use suction cups to suck out increased ill pressures in the body – especially in the lungs – to eliminate the sickness. The cups thus leave marks on the skin which were interpreted as abuse marks by the doctor. By his intervention, my colleague cleared the confusion; got the child proper treatment and the relieved family went home together. Such confusions exist in many of our intertwining, mixing and confused worlds.

Many immigrants who move here were farmers or ranchers back in their homeland before migrating here and most likely will move to the rural areas of our nation to continue their vocation. They may feel alienated and keep their problems to themselves – especially medical issues – till it is too late. We need to be cognizant of our environment as it has never been more dynamic than it is today. And in no place is the confusion of miscommunication more perilous than in medicine. New communication tools can help us overcome these barriers, especially in the rural areas of our country with limited access to language translators.

WATERING HOLE

The birds this morning massed on the tree above the water trough we keep for our animals. A large flock of robins, noisily announcing their arrival.

Fresh water is scarce in the mountains of America's desert southwest. Watering holes of any kind attract all kinds of wild life. I can count on seeing wild horses, deer, birds, wasps and bees visiting the trough throughout the day. On one occasion, a rather large tarantula stopped over for a drink. This morning's congregation noisily took turns quenching their thirst while others kept a worried eye out for our cats. When resources are in short supply, all creatures – man and beast – will take chances to survive. We should remember that a shrinking watering hole attracts more needy not less. Denying them what they need is a transgression.

The resilience of mankind, however, has always found ways to overcome adversity. Optimism dictates to be persevering in our ways and work toward improving and correcting deficiencies. A news bit a while back got my attention that truly shows this resiliency. A program called, "*Superhero Boost,*" pairs children with disabilities with designers and engineers to create custom prosthetics like an arm that shoots glitter or plastic snakes and shows that anything is possible. The program empowers kids by helping them create 'superhero' prosthetics. In the process they learn some pretty cool tools and technology (like 3D printing, robotics or AI) and working alongside professional designers, engineers and makers opens up an entire world of possibilities that was unknown to them.

Such ideologies abound around the world. All that is needed is a chance to put them to work. By providing the means and opportunities to the disadvantaged, a prosperous world will be created. After all, the main reason people leave their homeland is in search of such prospects. If opportunities came to them rather than them going after it, there would not be a reason for migration. And if instead of selling arms to governments we empowered their people with knowledge and tools to care for themselves, we could witness a better world in transition. Doctors, scientists, architects, designers and engineers could be paired up with young people through new communication tools and provide them the means to use them. Paraphrasing Superhero Boost's motto, by *rethinking disadvantage as a great opportunity for rebuilding society,* many problems could be defeated.

Many charitable organizations ask people to support a child in a third world country. Now think how wonderful it would be if professionals adopt a child in these places and teach them the basics of their profession – no money needed. A doctor could teach someone about healthcare, an engineer on how to fix or build needed machinery or an architect sharing knowledge of how to build or repair a dwelling, road, sewer, etc. Such prospects and scenarios are endless. It can all be done through the power of Internet from the safety of one's home or office. Let's make a difference. By giving them water, they will not amass around the neighbor's watering hole.

THOMAS EDISON

On October 21, 1879, Thomas Edison figured out a workable electric light bulb. It is amazing that the discovery and invention of usable electricity is just a little over a hundred years old. Yet since it's invention, we have moved light years ahead in every aspect of our lives. From transportation to communication, in science and technology, agriculture and medicine, so on and so on. It has irreversibly and irrevocably changed man's destiny in the cosmos. We have moved so fast and so far that much of it seems a blur.

I grew up without electricity. Electricity first came to our town when I was fourteen years old. I clearly remember that day, and I remember my grandmother's reaction to it. When I turned the switch on in our house for the first time, she shivered and said "That is the work of the devil." She was not the only person who told me that. Decades later, when I was working on the island of Dominica in the Caribbean, I met an old Carib Indian man who refused to have electricity in his house, claiming it was evil and would drain his soul. A similar concern, I heard from an elderly Navajo woman once. Of course such superstitions may be unfounded and baseless, but can we ignore the fact that electricity has propelled us so far past our traditions, beliefs, and even faith that we look at the world around us with such vision and mind that could make us forget our roots.

In our zeal to move faster and faster into the future, we must keep in mind that unless humanity moves forward together, those in the front may become so separated from the others that we may completely lose sight of each other. That would be a calamity neither group can afford. Fortunately the tools are here for us all to advance together. We just need to use them.

My entire life as an adult has been spent in healthcare, so I can only speak of this arena. Here I see technology that can provide us with opportunities and solutions to keep us all healthy as we move forward. Let us use this gift against illness, disease, poverty and illiteracy. If we keep our people – *all people* – educated, healthy and well cared for, moving forward for the entire humanity would be a good possibility. I think that would please Thomas Edison very much.

OF WITCHES, LA LLORONAS, SUPERSTITIONS AND TRADITIONS

All the conditions were right for a spooky Halloween that year. An early winter storm was blowing snow flurries in the Capital City, and a near full moon adding to the drama. People dashing home to get out of the cold indicated that it may be a quiet evening. I had arrived home early and was looking to a restful evening not expecting to have any Trick or Treaters due to the weather. So my surprise to hear a knock on the door, followed by a child's voice *Trick or treat!*

What kind of parent would let their kid out on a night like this, I wondered.

I lived in a courtyard type of apartment compound and the many dwellings around the protected yard created a secure environment for the children. So even on a night like this, tradition trumped the weather and all sorts of costumed creatures appeared at my door. Often their parents stood by the gate while their kids called on the homes.

As the night matured, it became more interesting. Once the young kids went home, teenagers and later, young adults showed up with bizarre and often risqué costumes. It was my first Halloween in the City Difference (as Santa Fe, NM is known) and I was surprised to see that age was not an issue with the young at heart and followers of tradition. The wind had died down and the sky cleared a bit. Thus, the temperature dropped and got bone chillingly cold. Around nine, people stopped knocking on my door, but the party at the dwelling across the yard became louder and more jovial. I looked out the window to see that people were dashing in and out of many of my neighbors and realized it was a celebration by everyone in the complex. I saw a neighbor approaching. As she was about to knock on my door, I opened it, she smiled and said, "No tricks, just treats." and handed me a glass of margarita. "Come, join the party." And opened her robe to reveal a painted body. "I am a mermaid, come see me in water." And laughed to my surprise. Realizing that I was not going to get any rest, I joined the party – and a wild one it was.

Close to midnight however, things took a turn. There was a commotion across the yard, and I was summoned to go see a guest who had become sick and was vomiting blood. A very young and frail girl was doubled over in pain and crying. She had thrown up a little and there was some questionable blood present. I asked her about history of ulcers, and her answer puzzled me, "Not before Zozobra." I suggested calling an ambulance but since the hospital was just a few blocks away a friend of hers drove her to the ER. The next day, I found out that she was checked, ulcers ruled out, and sent home with instructions to take Pepto-Bismol and avoid alcohol.

The next morning got as noisy and animated as the previous evening as many tried to sort themselves out as to where they were and where they belonged. It seemed that a few of the guests found themselves waking not at their own place. Several conversations were going on simultaneously in the courtyard and I heard Zozobra mentioned, so I inquired as what it had to do with the young lady's illness.

Well, it seemed that our friend was at the burning of Zozobra (a New Mexico tradition since 1920s), the month before and claims that her boisterous dancing at the event attracted the attention of an old woman, whom she called la llorona, who gave her the evil eye and ever since, she's been having stomach issues.

That event brings back to mind another incident. Almost a decade later to date, I was covering the ER in a Northern New Mexico town when two very attractive young blonds in risqué witch costumes were brought in by the local police for asthma attack. The young ladies were sisters with a long history of asthma. They were from out of town, visiting friends on Halloween and due to too much drinking and smoking at the party found themselves in trouble. Their inhalers just were not doing the trick, and they called for help. Since no ambulance was readily available, a town policeman brought them, in his police car. At the ER, their presence attracted the attention of several people in the waiting area, and a quarrel broke out between them and the police officer who had brought the ladies in. In the scuffle, the officer tried to Mace one of the unruly, only to Mace himself by accident. The chaos that pursued became a gossip around the small town that was talked about and got more bizarre with the passing of time.

Fortunately, that event too had a positive ending as both young witches responded well to our treatment and left town the next day.

June 6, 1966 was yet another day I remember. It was a Monday and since I worked on the weekends, it was my day off. I got a call early that morning however, and was offered double pay, if I would go to work. Once there, I found out that many had called in sick due to the day being 6/6/66. I was familiar with the significance of the number as it is rooted from the Book of Revelation in the Bible but learned quite a bit more that day. Though many of my coworkers were Jewish, our hospital – where I worked – still received enough sick calls to make it necessary to call in additional help. I was surprised to learn that some of those who stayed home that day were doctors, nurses and other highly educated people.

Much of such superstitious beliefs are what we are taught as a child and are ingrained in our thinking. They are not easy to ignore or overcome no matter what level of education or social class we gain. Many of our presidents, for example were superstitious. George Washington, Harry Truman, George W. Bush, Franklin D. Roosevelt, John F. Kennedy, Abraham Lincoln, Ulysses S. Grant, Donald Trump, and others all had credulous beliefs. Ronald Reagan even hired an astrologer to help with his daily schedules. Many of us ourselves have quirky ideas.

New Mexico with its rich Indian, Spanish, and Anglo ethnicities has countless traditions, rituals, folklore and legends. Many intertwine and create new versions of the old tales. Tales that are unique to certain cultures, new tales that come about from cultural interactions and some tales still in the making which add to the colorful customs. An interesting aspect of such tales is the health concerns linked to them, some good and others not. Curses, evil eyes, and ill wishes are very real to many and whether science agrees or believes in them or not, they have a profound and weighty established presence. As healthcare professionals, we need to be aware of such beliefs and address them if needed. Understanding of such thinking strengthens our relationships, builds trust and helps with better communication with our patients, thus making us a much better healthcare provider. Not to mention it adding flavor to life itself.

BOB HOOVER

We lost one of my idols, the legendary pilot R.A. "Bob" Hoover in October 2016. He was 94. With his trademark panama hat and Tennessee drawl, Hoover was an icon of American aviation.

Many of us in aviation held him as a hero in many ways. His love and devotion to flying was second to none and he was an avid promoter of it. He flew in more than 2,500 civilian and military air shows in the U.S. and around the world, thrilling those on the ground with his trademark routine: shutting off the engines on his Aero-Commander while performing loops and dives. He flew with such precision that he was able to pour ice tea into a glass in the middle of a barrel roll. After every air show, Hoover would take time to talk to the young people and promote flying. Hoover attended an air show in Santa Fe, NM in 1998. I took my son there and met the legendary flier. He was more interested in talking to my then seven year old son than to me.

Hoover's achievements are too numerous to list here, but what he did for aviation could be a great lesson for all of us in medicine. For while he flew for more than seventy years of his life, his focus was always on promoting aviation and helping to make it safer and more resourceful.

Every pilot faces a potential emergency requiring a forced landing off an airport on every flight. Calamities happen when the pilot panics and stops flying the plane, becoming a passenger himself. Bob used to say; "When faced with a forced landing, fly the airplane as far through the crash as possible!" A lesson I have carried throughout many aspects of my life.

In healthcare too, we face the potential of errors, but should never forget our primary role of serving the ill and the injured and serving them wherever they are – in rural as well as urban areas. Just as GPS makes navigating the skies a lot easier than guessing where in God's sky we are, new communication tools make better practice of medicine possible as well. It should be our resolution to practice good and safe medicine as Bob did flying airplanes. Rest in peace Bob, you will not be forgotten.

NOVEMBER

Of Note in November

November 1, 1848 – The first medical school for women opened in Boston. In 1874, the school merged with the Boston University School of Medicine, becoming one of the first coed medical schools.

November 3, 1839 – The first Opium War between China and Britain began after British frigates blew up several Chinese junks.

November 7, 1867 (1934) – Marie Curie was born in Warsaw, Poland. In 1903, she and her husband received the Nobel Prize for physics for their discovery of the element Radium.

November 8, 1656 (1742) – Astronomer and mathematician Edmund Halley was born in London.

November 8, 1895 – X-rays (electromagnetic rays) were discovered by Wilhelm Roentgen at the University of Wuerzburg in Germany.

November 8, 1922 (2001) – Christiaan Barnard was born in Beaufort West, Cape of Good Hope Province, South Africa. He performed the first human heart transplant in 1967.

November 10, 1775 – The U.S. Marine Corps was established as part of the U.S. Navy. It became a separate unit on July 11, 1789.

November 11th – Celebrated as Veterans Day in the U.S.

November 15, 1777 – The Articles of Confederation were adopted by Continental Congress.

November 15, 1864 – During the American Civil War, Union troops under General William T. Sherman burned the city of Atlanta.

November 15, 1887 (1986) – Georgia O'Keeffe was born in Sun Prairie, Wisconsin. She painted desert landscapes and flower studies. She lived in New Mexico for most of her life.

November 17, 1790 (1868) – German mathematician August Mobius was born in Schulpforte, Germany. He was a pioneer in topology, the study of geometric figures that remain constant even when twisted or distorted.

November 17, 1869 – After 10 years of construction, the Suez Canal was formally opened.

November 17, 1993 – NAFTA, the North American Free Trade Agreement was approved by the U.S. House of Representatives.

November 18, 1789 (1851) – Photography inventor Louis Daguerre was born in Cormeilles, France. In 1839, he invented a process that produced lasting pictures.

November 18, 1883 – A Connecticut schoolteacher, Charles F. Dowd, proposed a uniform time zone plan for the U.S. consisting of four zones.

November 20, 1858 (1940) – Swedish author Selma Lagerlof was born in Varmland Province. She was a member of the Swedish Academy and in 1909 became the first woman to receive the Nobel Prize for literature.

November 20, 1889 (1953) – Astronomer Edwin Hubble was born in Marshfield, Missouri. He pioneered the concept of an expanding universe.

November 26, 1607 (1638) – Harvard College founder John Harvard was born in London.

November 26, 1789 – The first American holiday was celebrated, proclaimed by President George Washington to be Thanksgiving Day.

November 26, 1832 (1919) – Mary Edwards Walker, physician and women's rights advocate, was born in Oswego, New York. She was the first female surgeon in U.S. Army, serving during the Civil War. In 1865, she became the first and only woman ever to receive the Medal of Honor.

November 27, 1701 (1744) – Anders Celsius was born in Sweden. He invented the centigrade (Celsius) temperature scale commonly used around the world.

November 29, 1898 (1963) – C.S. Lewis was born in Belfast, Ireland (as Clive Staples Lewis). He wrote many books on Christian teachings.

November 30, 1835 (1910) – Samuel Clemens was born in Florida, Missouri. He wrote books under the pen name Mark Twain.

CULTURES OF THE PAST,
CULTURES OF THE FUTURE

Not long ago, practitioners of different disciplines were discriminated against. The hierarchy ended with the MDs on top of the pecking order. Even the graduates of different medical institutions ranked in a special roster of their own. Graduates of foreign schools were looked at with suspicion and tested rigorously. DOs were considered second-class practitioners not worthy of sharing the same institutions with MDs – they had their own hospitals, boards, organizations etc. Chiropractors and Podiatrists were considered wannabe orthopedic surgeons, optometrists wannabe ophthalmologists, on and on and on.

I suppose that we have 'for profit medicine' to thank for incorporating some of the different disciplines into their managed care system. Though their aspiration may have been to tap into the money being spent in those arenas.

Internet changed much of that as information of the logic, advocacy, rationale, and applicability of these different disciplines became available and we learned that each doctrine has it's own value and can and does complement others. Today one can receive acupuncture treatments in the orthopedist's office, massage therapy in the chiropractor's practice and even leeches are used by some surgeons in place of lancing boils.

What has changed? Was it the capitalistic desire to keep all the health-care money under one umbrella? Was it that we have really become that open-minded or is something else at work here? Whatever it is, it is propelling us toward a new culture. As internet further expands the boundaries of our practice, some of us take our old ideologies with us and defend them. Others take their newfound attitudes and opinions and spread them around. Chaos may pursue in arenas slow to change and confusion where there is too much change. How to cope with it all and how to ensure the safety of our patients will be an issue that needs noticing and safeguarding. Finding the right balance may be difficult but the alternative could be pandemonium. Adding to all of this is the demands of a mobile society wanting to take everything with them. Which makes establishing a sound foundation for Telehealth and Telemedicine of paramount importance. It behooves us to build the new paradigm of healthcare on a sound and firm basis. An old saying states that; "If the first brick is placed crooked, to the stars the wall continues crooked!" In the zeal of getting on the bandwagon, many are implementing dubious and even impractical models. Let's be cognizant of building a level foundation for the future culture of our healthcare system.

MUSIC FOR THE WOUNDED

Despite the dark picture many paint of our time, the humanity and com-passion of people always surfaces in times of need and disasters. Resiliency, audacity, courage and bravery set apart the can-doers from others. It's inter-esting how music always becomes a major healer in such events. When hurricane Katrina devastated the gulf region, returning colleagues from the area told of the musicians gathering in the evening hours and jamming in the dark and flooded streets. People would assemble and dance, chasing their fears away.

I was visiting colleagues on a reservation several years ago when a big and deadly sandstorm rolled through. Afterward I witnessed the native people finding the injured and the dead, caring for the wounded and bury-ing the deceased. To my amazement, after grief, cries, and prayer, they took out their drums and instruments and started playing. Teary-eyed men and women sang and danced well into the night. I don't remember why but I started walking away from the site and into the desert. The further I went, the more the music changed. It seemed to wrap itself around the dunes and roll down the hills, soothing the very sand and air that a few hours earlier was wrecking havoc on the desert.

After an earthquake in Central America, all the news was of devasta-tion and death. While reporting from a hospital packed with hurting injured, I noticed a couple behind the reporter, playing their guitars – comforting the wounded.

And after the recent hurricane in Puerto Rico, an old friend called from Mayagüez to report that she and her family were OK. She further spoke of how every night the dark streets of the city come alive with music, dancing and singing. Similar stories of endurance and compassion are everywhere.

If Music is the universal language, Medicine is the universal vocation. Just as one can strap a guitar and travel the world and be listened to, a medical vocation of any kind would be welcomed all over the world. The need for healthcare is universal. We do not hurt in Spanish or Chinese. Diabetes does not have shades of French or Indian. Our children don't cry in Swahili or Portuguese. We are welcomed and our services sought after because there is a need. Music provides healing powers to our soul and spirit as physical medicine does our bodies. In many parts of the world, lacking amenities of the modern time, communities pull together and deal with the damaged lives and homes without outside help. Many smaller isolated towns or islands don't ever receive help from any government, nor do they even expect it. Our dependence on technological advances though, has handicapped us. Today lack of electricity, functioning plumbing, access to medical clinics, etc. delays recovery efforts for many in this twenty first century world.

Luckily, our profession has established many ways to respond to medical needs of affected areas. We may not be able to do much about electricity and plumbing but we have made great strides in providing healthcare. That gives us hope and adds to our resiliency and survivability. Just as Brahms, Beethoven or Rodriguez sooth the senses equally in Europe, Asia or Africa, our medical ability eases the discomfort of many everywhere. And we can depend on our musician colleagues to calm the situation while we do our work – THANK YOU!

WORLD ANTIBIOTIC AWARENESS WEEK

In November, we are informed of World Antibiotic Awareness week. It is amazing that antibiotics are not even a hundred years old and yet we have developed, expanded and used them to such levels that many diseases are now resistant to them. Is this due to our lack of full knowledge of them, over availability, or the financial gain of the manufacturers of these products? Many reports seem to indicate that places with less access to these drugs harbor healthier populations. In our overactive and rushed societies, we are often forced to act against our better judgment. Like most providers, I too had my share of anxious mothers who demanded a coarse of antibiotics for their sick child, not because the child needed it but because the mother desperately stated that, "she couldn't afford to miss work." For many years though, people did just fine without these wonder drugs. Even today many do well without them.

I was working on a small island in the Caribbean many years ago. When I first got to the island, a child of 11 years of age was referred to me who had suffered a fall resulting in a compound (open) fracture of his elbow. The wound was a week old and contaminated. I admitted him and ordered IV antibiotics. The next morning, while making my rounds, I saw no notes regarding the ordered meds. The response to my inquiry was; "OK".

"What do you mean OK?" I asked the nurse. "Has this child had his meds or not?"

"NO!" was the answer. "And why not," I asked somewhat irate.

"We don't have any antibiotics." Was the answer. It was revealed that no antibiotics of any kind existed on the island. "When ship come," I was told, "maybe he bring medicine." There was no telling when the ship would come.

I remember my Grandmother would allow flies to lay their eggs in such wounds and the resulting larva would eat the puss. The child's mother told me that the local medicine man had made the same kind of a suggestion but she had brought him to us to receive modern care. Of course I, being the representative of the American medical establishment, couldn't suggest maggots. In the end an Indian physician working on the island came to my rescue. He applied Plaster of Paris bandages to the elbow without any padding. The cast not only immobilized the elbow, the plaster acted as a wick and sucked the puss out, healing the wound. When I left the island several months later, the child's elbow had healed and he had fairly good range of motion. It then behooves us to keep the old practices alive. More and more, it is being discovered that there still is a viable integrity to their use. Including the use of maggots and leeches. Before the discovery of antibiotics, they worked for thousands of years – they still do.

The efforts by the UN and WHO has had some positive results and fortunately many of us are heeding the warnings and are cognizant of the way we practice. But it is not enough to educate ourselves to the proper use of these drugs. It becomes even more important to educate our patients and overcome their suspicion of our change in treating them. Particularly in established, older patients who for many years have been receiving antibiotics from us for even minor colds and flu. Especially since they can still get these drugs from some of our other colleagues who are either too tired to fight these patients, too ignorant or just financially motivated. As practitioners, our judgments are our own and unless some harm shows itself, no one really questions our rational. The problem here is that harm may show itself years later and no one will go back to see who was the culprit. Maybe we should be our colleague's keepers and educators. But that packs in its own set of ramifications and ethical questions.

While I was working in a resort town, many of my patients and even residents of the town had permanent addresses elsewhere. So, although I was their regular provider there, they considered their doctors back home as their primary care physician.

One such patient was the wife of a local businessman. She brought her young baby to see me once. The baby had been running a low grade fever and pulling on her ears. The mother stated that the baby had another ear infection and that her doctor back home usually prescribed antibiotics. I examined the baby and found no evidence of any kind of infection. I told her so and suggested that we should treat her symptomatically. She became argumentative and said that her doctor back home always gives her an antibiotic. I tried to reason with her but she left disappointed.

Our town pharmacy was next door and later that afternoon I saw her in there filling a prescription. Later I asked our pharmacist and was told that a prescription for antibiotics was called in from an out of town doctor for her baby.

Today there is more awareness of these types of problems and technology provides us with tools that can be used to overcome some of these misunderstandings. Proper use of new communication tools can reduce or even eliminate many ambiguities and help us make an accurate diagnosis, even when our patients are away. There really is no excuse for practices such as the one described above.

BLESSED THANKSGIVING

November is when we celebrate Thanksgiving – my favorite holiday in America. In the spirit of the occasion, let's consider this prayer from the elders of many cultures, including our Native Americans. For appreciation and respect of nature and it's way of life leads to protecting it and thus a healthier environment for ourselves. Let us pray:

Oh Great Creator
Whose voice I hear in the wind and running waters
Whose beauty I see in flowers and the setting sun
Whose breath I feel in all living creatures
Whose warmth I sense in the heart of my children
Myself, my parents and their parents before them.

Hear my thankful prayers
Thankful for the nature that keeps me alive
Thankful for the teachings of all your prophets
Thankful for the order of your universe
Thankful for the knowledge of all your creation
That allows me to see beyond what can't be seen.

Oh Great Creator
Give me the wisdom to see my insignificants
Give me the wisdom to realize the fragility of existence
Give me the wisdom to comprehend the balance of nature

Give me the wisdom to discern right from wrong
So that I can add to your blessings and not take away from them.

Oh Great Creator hear my prayers
Guide me toward that which is the right path
Guide me to know my limits
Guide me to not harm all things that I can see and not see
Guide me to rise above my ignorance
And see that all mankind are my kin
That without them I am nothing
My very existence meaningless.

I pray so when I come before you
My hands and heart will be clean
And I can stand tall and without shame.

SONGS AND GUNS

"Amado mio," sang the pretty señorita to the music of Bossa Nova. The hypnotic rhythm of the Spanish music had everyone gyrating in their seats.

We were gathered for Thanksgiving and on the weekend following the feast, my son took us to hear the Latin Jazz and burn some of the extra calories we had piled up. The lounge was crowded and the cacophony of languages being spoken added to the exotic atmosphere of the place. It was heart warming and exciting to see how the diverse cultures gathered in such a place had no differences of opinion and swayed to the music in unison.

A group of Asian people caught my attention. A friend, who has lived in Japan and South Korea, informed us that they were businessmen from South Korea there with their wives and hosts enjoying the evening. Looking at the serenity of the mix of cultures present made me wonder why we have fought so many wars in the world.

An absurd idea hit me, maybe if they played this music on those battlefields, people would have put away their guns and dance their differences away. I don't know, maybe it was the margaritas.

Differences that we try to resolve by aggression, affect our health and well-being, as well as the structure of our world. Innocent people often get caught in these struggles. When emotional or physical injuries occur, they seek our help. Healthcare providers are then caught in their own quagmire of having to deal with the problem.

A while back, I was serving with the Red Cross in response to a short civil war in Jordan that left many injured. Although we had nothing to do with the conflict, as Americans, we were the focus of hostility by one of the groups in the conflict. So much that we could not care for them adequately. We resolved the problem by sending the injured from that group to the much smaller group of the Swedish Red Cross, and had them consult us on their care.

Today of course new communication tools gives us what we need to care for many of our friends and adversaries alike. Only if we can keep politics out of our mind while caring for the ones under our care. Is that too much wishful thinking and desire?

REFUGEES FOR CONGRESS

Perhaps the best reason for running for US Congress was given by Ilhan Omar of Minnesota, the first refugee ever elected to Congress;

> *I did not expect to come to the United States and go to school with kids who were worried about food as much as I was worried about it in a refugee camp.*

Unfortunately, that is the state of the economy for many people in developed countries as well as the developing ones. Which portrays the confusing state of our world. What makes it even more perplexing is the fact that so many politicians seem to be totally disconnected from this reality and cannot even relate to it. This Escherian duality and parallel and disjointed veracity feeds the fires of discontent and restlessness.

As I have mentioned in the introduction to this chapter, I share M.C. Escher's outlook on life as a duality. Escher believed that there is an opposite to everything and every situation. It's not so much as one being better than the other, but rather two sides of the same coin (so to speak). What we do with the side we find ourselves on, is what makes the outcome desirable or objectionable. In this duality, while one person may live in total chaos and gloom another can live in the same world and under the same situation and circumstances but be totally content and happy. So it is that people are often caught in the ironic situation of being represented by those who cannot fathom their predicament or understand it.

Whether it's the inability to find food, medicine, proper healthcare, or shelter – no matter the place – the end result is suffering. Yet, through the use of technology, one can see the availability of all that is out of reach – adding to the mayhem.

Making the job of the healthcare providers evermore difficult is the fact that even when medical care is available, it is often too costly for many. Which brings us back to the confusing state of today's politics. The new elections in America and around the world are giving new hope to people on one side of the spectrum, while making the other side upset, adding to the polarization. But the true reason is that with so much conflicting information, most people don't even understand the issues and are just taking sides.

If we are to truly appreciate the predicament of people in the many camps around the world, we must first be aware of it in our own society. Then perhaps we can understand the plight of others. And here is where refugees, like Ilhan Omar, can teach us a lot!

TWO DOLLARS
FOR A DREAM?

Money in hand, they stood in line by the hundreds. To buy tickets of chance. A chance to dream for a few days or hours in hope of becoming rich.

It is human nature; I suppose, to take a chance to improve ones life, destiny, future. Even the rich – those who don't need to – often take chances to increase their holdings, their prospects and their fortunes, by starting new ventures, new businesses, new investments. So it is understandable to see that when the future is uncertain, opportunities invisible, and prospects stagnant, leaving the tentative for a chance of better would be justified.

Sacrifices made by athletes, sports car drivers, aerobatic pilots, explorers, mountain climbers and the like are all testament to the audacity of mankind in the dream of improving their skill, art and life. At times, even at the cost of their health and life.

I once witnessed the tragic death of an aviation friend when he flew his aircraft into the ground at an air-show. He flew his aerobatic maneuvers close to the ground. Many of us objected to his carelessness. But he used to say that his audience was on the ground and so he needed to be close to them. On the fateful day he was about to finish his air-show with a loop. We all gasped as he entered the loop too close to the ground. On the role out, he ran out of air space and flew into the ground coming to stop with a frightening thud. I ran to him, but as I got close, slowed down to catch my breath when I saw him sitting in the open cockpit smiling. I thought that he had miraculously survived the crash. But as others and I reached him, it became clear that he was not with us anymore.

The many abandoned pueblos of the Native Americans of the Southwest are also a testament to the search for a better life. Despite the incredible resourcefulness used in building them, many were vacated due to environmental, political or other unknown reasons. When it came time to seek a better life, they cast off all their work and security and migrated to new places in the dream of finding something better. Just like the many migrants of today.

Healthcare too, is one area mankind takes chances. New medication, devices, treatment techniques, and new places to receive them are all evidence of the importance we place on it. In our profession, we have witnessed implausible advances in all aspects of the medical field. Whether it is DNA Specific Drugs, Robotic Surgeries, or Telehealth and Telemedicine. It is a wondrous and exciting time of history we live in. Many dreams are coming true so it's worth dreaming more, hoping more and taking chances for that betterness. Whether by starting a new job or venture, or moving to a new land or country, or spending two dollars for a lottery ticket and that dream of richness.

DECEMBER

Of Note in December

December 1, 1955 – Rosa Parks was arrested in Montgomery, Alabama, for refusing to give up her seat to a white man. Her arrest resulted in a year long boycott of the city bus system by African-Americans.

December 1, 1988 – Benazir Bhutto was nominated to become prime minister of Pakistan, the first woman to govern a Muslim nation.

December 1, 1994 – The head of the U.N. Commission on Rwanda estimated 500,000 deaths had resulted from genocide.

December 2, 1823 – President James Monroe introduced his "Monroe Doctrine", prohibiting colonization of the American continents by European powers.

December 2, 1942 – Physicists led by Enrico Fermi carried out the world's first successful nuclear chain reaction at the University of Chicago.

December 2, 1971 – The United Arab Emirates was formed by seven Arab kingdoms of Abu Dhabi, Dubai, Sharjah, Ajman, Umm al Qaiwain and Fujairah.

December 2, 1982 – The first permanent artificial heart was implanted in 61year-old Barney C. Clark by Dr. William De Vries at the University of Utah Medical Center in Salt Lake City. Clark survived 112 days after the implantation.

December 3, 1967 – The first successful heart transplant was performed by Dr. Christiaan Barnard at Cape Town, South African, on Louis Washkansky, who lived for 18 days.

December 3, 1984 – A deadly gas leak (of methyl isocyanate) at a Union Carbide plant in Bhopal, India, killed at least 3,000 persons and injured more than 200,000.

December 4, 1829 – The British banned the practice of "suttee" in India in which Indian females traditionally burned themselves to death on their husband's funeral pyre.

December 5, 1782 (1862) – Martin van Buren the 8th U.S. President was born in Kinderhook, New York. He was the first President who was born a citizen of the United States.

December 5, 1933 – The 18th Amendment (Prohibition Amendment) to the U.S. Constitution was repealed.

December 6, 1865 – The 13th Amendment to the U.S. Constitution was ratified abolishing slavery.

December 6, 1877 – Thomas Edison spoke the children's verse "Mary had a Little Lamb..." while demonstrating his newly invented phonograph.

December 8, 1765 (1825) – Eli Whitney was born in Westboro, Massachusetts. His invention of Cotton gin had a big impact on the economy of the South. By 1800, cotton production increased from 3,000 bales a year to about 73,000.

December 8, 1991 – The USSR (Union of Soviet Socialist Republics) ceased to exist, as the leaders of Russia, Byelorussia and the Ukraine signed an agreement creating the Commonwealth of Independent States.

December 9, 1886 (1956) – Clarence Birdseye was born in Brooklyn, New York. He developed a method of deep freezing foods and was one of the founders of General Foods Corp.

December 9, 1948 – The United Nations General Assembly unanimously approved the Convention on the Prevention and Punishment of the Crime of Genocide. It took effect on January 12, 1951, following ratification by 20 member nations.

December 10, 1787 (1851) – Thomas Gallaudet was born in Philadelphia, Pennsylvania. He was one of the founders of the American School for the Deaf in Hartford, Connecticut, in 1817.

December 10, 1896 – Swedish chemist Alfred Nobel died at San Remo, Italy. His will stipulated that income from his estate be used for awards recognizing those who have made valuable contributions to humanity. Prizes for Peace, Physics, Chemistry, Medicine, Literature and Economics are presented annually, on the anniversary of his death.

December 10, 1948 – The Universal Declaration of Human Rights was adopted by the General Assembly at the UN.

December 11, 1901 – The first transatlantic radio signal was transmitted by Guglielmo Marconi from Cornwall, England, to St. John's, Newfoundland.

December 14, 1503 (1566) – Physician Nostradamus was born in St. Remy, Provence, France (as Michel de Notredame). He wrote astrological predictions in rhymed quatrains, believed by many to foretell the future.

December 14, 1962 – The Mariner II space probe sent information from the planet Venus, the first ever received from another planet.

December 15, 1770 (1827) – Ludwig van Beethoven was born in Bonn, Germany.

December 15, 1791 – The Bill of Rights became effective.

December 15, 1832 (1923) – Alexandre Eiffel was born in Dijon, France. He designed the Eiffel Tower for the Paris International Exposition of 1889.

December 15, 1993 – The GATT (General Agreement on Tariffs and Trade) Treaty was approved by delegations from 117 countries. The treaty was designed to reduce international tariffs, eliminate trade quotas, and protect intellectual property.

December 17, 1903 – Orville and Wilbur Wright achieved the first powered flight near Kitty Hawk, North Carolina.

December 21st – Winter solstice in the Northern Hemisphere. In the Southern Hemisphere today is the beginning of summer.

December 21, 1846 – Anesthesia (ether) was used for the first time by Robert Liston during a leg amputation, in England.

December 23, 1913 – The U.S. Congress established the Federal Reserve System to serve as the nation's central bank.

December 23, 1947 – The transistor was invented at Bell Laboratories by John Bardeen, Walter Brattain and William Shockley. They shared the Nobel Prize for their invention.

December 24, 1745 (1813) – Benjamin Rush was born in Byberry, Pennsylvania. He was a doctor and humanitarian; whose writings on mental illness earned him the title "Father of Psychiatry." He was one of the first doctors to describe alcoholism as a chronic disease.

December 25th – Christmas Day, commemorating the birth of Jesus of Nazareth. Although the exact date of his birth is not known, it has been celebrated on December 25th by the Roman Catholic Church since 336 A.D.

December 25, 1642 (1727) – Isaac Newton was born in Woolsthorpe, Lincolnshire, England. He was a mathematician, scientist and author, best known for his work *Philosophiae Naturalis Principia Mathematica* on the theory of gravitation.

December 25, 1821 (1912) – Clara Barton was born in Oxford, Massachusetts. She served as a nurse during the Civil War and in 1881 founded the American Red Cross.

December 26, 1893 (1976) – Mao TseTung was born in Hunan Province, China. He was a Chinese librarian, teacher and communist revolutionist, considered the "founding father" of the People's Republic of China.

December 26, 2004 – A magnitude 9.3 earthquake on the seafloor of the Indian Ocean set off a series of giant tsunamis, killing an estimated 230,000 people with another 1.5 million left homeless. The tidal waves hit the shorelines of many countries including Indonesia, Sri Lanka, Thailand, India and Somalia.

December 27, 1571 (1630) – Johannes Kepler was born in Wurttemberg, Germany. He is considered to be the father of modern astronomy.

December 27, 1822 (1895) – Louis Pasteur was born in Dole, France. He developed the pasteurization process to kill harmful bacteria with heat and found ways of preventing silkworm disease, anthrax, chicken cholera, and rabies.

December 27, 1831 – Charles Darwin set out from Plymouth, England, aboard the ship *HMS Beagle* on his fiveyear global scientific expedition. In 1859, he published *"The Origin of Species by Means of Natural Selection."*

December 27, 1945 – The International Monetary Fund was established in Washington, D.C.

December 30, 1993 – Israel and the Vatican signed an agreement on mutual recognition, seeking to end 2,000 years of unfriendly Christian Jewish relations.

December 31, 1879 – Thomas Edison provided the first demonstration of his electric lamp at his laboratory in Menlo Park, New Jersey.

December 31st – New Year's Eve, the final evening of the Gregorian calendar year, traditionally a night for merrymaking to welcome in the new year.

TIME MERCHANTS

As we finish the age-old celebration of Thanksgiving and prepare ourselves for Christmas and the coming New Year, I cannot help to wonder on the immortality of Time itself. For whatever time is, its hold on us is dictatorial and constant. And nowhere is this demand more critical than in medicine. Despite its hold on every one of us individually, everyone wishes, demands and does everything to control it, and when it seems that time is running out, many turn to medicine to borrow, buy, squeeze or even steal more of it. But do we, as practitioners have any of it to bestow upon our patients? There are many who think we do.

I had a famous singer as a patient once and at another time a champion golfer. On both occasions, they became ill before a scheduled performance and wanted me to cure them immediately. "I don't have TIME to be sick," was the mutual statement. And how about the mother with a sick child who says; "I don't have the TIME to stay home with him." or someone with a sick parent asking; "Can't you put her in the hospital, I don't have the TIME to watch her." Are we truly merchants or bankers of time?

Then there are times when we ourselves are stretched for time, well beyond the given hours of the day. When we are late for surgery, or it is the end of the day and there are still ten patients waiting to be seen.

How many times have we said; "Only if there were more hours in the day!" But there isn't even one minute more in the God given day. Time has no prejudices of our race or creed, does not understand war or peace, and cares not for our wealth or lack of it. Despite all our rushing, sleep or food deprivation, and all of our multi-tasking, it moves on a steady and uninterrupted rhythm. Then one day we look in the mirror and say, "Where did the time go?"

Fortunately for us, technology has given us tools to manage our time better for the benefit of our patients and ourselves. Telecommunication cuts short the time we spend between our patients and the way we care for them. But only if we use it, and use it properly. Tomorrow, the sun will rise, the wind will blow, the tides come and go, and the moon and stars wander about us, as time marches on. But hopefully we will have time for a good night sleep. So as a lullaby I encourage you to listen to this song by Sandy Denny and sang by Nina Simone; "Who knows where the time goes" (its worthwhile to look this up and listen to it).

UNITING THE DIVIDED

"History is a sort of tangled web of contradictions. ..." said Robert Service, Professor of Russian History at Oxford University.

Because obviously we don't learn from history and no time in our history have contradictions been more noticeable than now. I suppose that we have the Internet and social media to thank for it. This tangled web of contradictions becomes more confusing when our leaders are the ones contributing to its propagation.

In the last century, after many wars, conflicts and global changes, many nations united in the hope of eliminating misunderstandings and confusion during conflicts and finding a way for an agreeable resolution. The UN Charter was signed on October 24, 1945, and the EU was founded on November 1, 1993, the African Union was founded on May 26, 2001, and the Union of South American Nations signed their charter on May 23, 2008. All to bolster the economic and political standing of their region. Ideas that make sense in philosophy and ideology, especially in today's mobile and interactive world. Yet the last few years have seen the demise of these principles. The meeting of the G20 (Dec. 2018) in Argentina was a testament to this madness. It seems that the leaders of G20 members had come to dismantle the whole unity of our world, rather than strengthen its accord. The real confusing fact is that these are the very countries that worked so hard to unite us in the first place. If history has taught us anything is that nationalism and individualism lead to disparity which leads to disagreements and conflict.

In no place do these contradictions cause more problems than in the task of providing healthcare. Our patients are supposed to be race-less, nation-less, and status-less human beings with a medical problem. We are not to judge them, but care for their health. It is hard however, to act and be neutral when they are forced to come to us, carrying race, nationality, legality and class flags. Such conditions prevent many from seeking help. Still at times, they risk coming to us at great expense to themselves, often to seek help for a loved one. I once cared for an illegal migrant who brought her sick child to be seen (see *IMMIGRANTS PLIGHT* in section two). Her apprehensive and anxious state disturbed me so much that I was concerned about her safety. Yet I could not recruit any help for her due to her lack of trust in me. Today there are many people like her and their suspicion of everyone is causing major problems. The squalid conditions under which many live adds to the dilemma. Consider the possibility of someone among them contacting a contagion and out of fear of getting caught, refusing to seek help. The infection may become a full-blown pandemic, spreading to the general population before we become aware of it.

New communication tools could help curb much of these short-comings. But only if those in power allow it to be implemented properly. Healthcare providers can demand it from their government to remove political hurdles from healthcare environments and allow us and our patients to keep the population healthy. After all, the last thing we need is to deport an individual with a serious contagion across a border to unsuspecting masses. It is cheaper to care for healthy people than sick – regardless of their legal status. Let's start uniting our fractured societies by caring for the sick and the injured – it is a humane thing to do!

BUBBLES

"Bubbles!" The little girl shouted with excitement swiping at the soap bubbles in front of her. But as other bubbles rose out of her reach, she became upset watching them float away. Her disabled body made it difficult to reach far. Soon she lost interest and pushed the hand holding the soap bottle away.

Her mother tried calming her; "Honey they are just playing with you."

"I don't want to play with something I can't hold or catch," she said tearfully.

She had MS (Multiple Sclerosis) and with the limited treatment options of the time, she was confined to bed or wheelchair. Many debilitating diseases had no treatment and the little knowledge available on their care was out of the reach of most healthcare providers.

Several years later, while serving in the US Air Force, I was a member of our unit's ATH (Air Transportable Hospital – Air Force's equivalent to Army's MASH unit). We were deployed to Amman, Jordan after the Jordanian Civil War in 1970. We treated many casualties of that war. But one young girl left a lasting memory. She had lost a leg in the bombing. We were trying to evaluate her, but her incessant screaming and crying made it difficult. At one point, I lost my temper and snapped at her that we were just trying to help her. "You want to help me," she shouted back, "take your bombs away and give me my leg back."

I was taken aback and felt terrible. Over the next couple of months, after many surgeries and skin grafts, we were able to save a short stump. I made friends with her and made her happy when I built her a prosthesis with a broom handle, before leaving Jordan.

Earlier in my military life, I had the good fortune of working with Dr. Eugene Thomas O'Brien who became a friend and mentor to me for many years. Dr. O'Brien was a hand surgeon in the United States Air Force. One of the best there was. His composed and peaceful mannerism calmed many chaotic and frustrating situations and his meticulous work and surgical techniques usually had marvelous outcomes.

Once, I was helping him apply a rather bulky dressing to a patient's wound in our clinic's large cast-room. I felt that the dressing was overdone and said; "This sticks out like the proverbial sore thumb." He quietly tapped me on the hand and pointed to the patient behind me. I turned to see another patient of ours who had lost both hands in an explosion in Vietnam. He held his bandaged arms up and in a chocked voice said; "Boy, how I wish for sore thumbs right now."

Diseases and wars have kept our profession very busy in the last hundred years. Today stories coming out of Iraq, Syria and Afghanistan bring back many unpleasant memories to people like myself. I am sure the medics of our armed forces have their hands full with all kinds of problems today. But if there is anything to be thankful about is that advances in communication technologies make it possible to bring help to our healthcare providers and patients in a timely fashion and allow sharing of ideas and treatment options with experts all around the world. Technologies have also advanced our treatment of diseases that were so debilitating not long ago. So much so that our little girl with MS can now live a more normal life. I hope and pray that we use these wonderful tools in our hands properly and not take them for granted. That we may be able to bring some sanity to our troubled world and find a peaceful way to live with each other.

PRESIDENCY OF CALVIN COOLIDGE

Calvin Coolidge gave the first presidential address that was broadcast on the radio on December 6, 1923. In less than a hundred years, we have moved from a simple radio broadcast to the astounding technology of communication that exists today. It was President Coolidge that helped create the Federal Radio Commission which has now evolved to become the Federal Communications Commission (FCC). While President Coolidge gave the first presidential address that was broadcast on radio, President Obama became the first president to hold virtual gatherings and town halls using Twitter, Facebook, LinkedIn, etc.

When I first entered the world of medicine in the ripe age of fourteen in the middle of the last century, we didn't even have anything that could be called technological to today's standard. Many of us grew up studying by candlelight and kerosene lamps. Electricity, radio, and even telephone were alien to many during our childhood. We had reusable needles and glass syringes, plaster of Paris came in powder form in a bucket, and x-ray machines stood in the corner of a room. We carried an alcohol lamp and sterilized the needle and syringes by boiling them in water before each use. When a patient was being x-rayed, usually his or her family was in the room with them, including their children. Antibiotics and vaccines were new and looked at with skepticism. We have come a long way in the past century. Today we consider all of the above archaic, old and even barbaric. Yet in their own time, they were state of the art medicine

In some ways our (my) generation has witnessed unprecedented history in the making. In one lifetime, we developed the technology that sent us to the moon and back, put a rover on Mars and had the Voyager spacecraft carry man's message beyond our solar system. Just recently, I was amused by a question from a young family member; "Uncle Reza, what is a phone booth?"

All the technology however has not made us wiser. It seems that the most advances are made in warfare and conflict creation. What a wonderful world would it be, if the "Military Industrial Complex" were changed into a "Health and Peace Development Complex." Today in healthcare as well as politics we have much ideology, dogma, and subjectivism, yet little objectivity, logic, and sensibility.

Coolidge was "distinguished for character more than for heroic achievement," wrote a democratic admirer, Alfred E. Smith. "His great task was to restore the dignity and prestige of the Presidency when it had reached the lowest ebb in our history ... in a time of extravagance and waste..." Sound familiar?

Before his death in January 1933, Coolidge confided to an old friend, " . . . I feel I no longer fit in with these times."

This too is something many of us can relate to! Still it is *us* who remember kerosene lamps and phone booths that must educate the younger generation of the rapid changes that our world is witnessing. By involving them, our young practitioners could benefit immensely in understanding, forecasting and developing the next generation of medical devices, medications and technologies. I for one would love to see younger people at our medical meetings, conferences and organizations – government and private. But I am consistently surprised to see how little attention is given to our needs by the newer generation. The future belongs to the young however and the better they understand the present, the better they could manage what is coming their way. After all yesterday wasn't that long ago! What would they say of today, sixty years from now, I wonder.

WRETCHED MASSES
AND BLESSED LOTS

The early morning fog wrapped its protective shroud around the harbor, city and ferry. A hidden mist hit the window of the moving ferry and slowly ran down the glass, distorting the scenery outside. The boat was traveling slower than usual, cautiously navigating the busy narrows.

I was standing by an open door, feeling the mist in my face and admiring the skill of the captain piloting the crowded boat in such weather. Somewhere in here is the Statue of Liberty, I thought. And as though by magic and on cue, the fog parted around the famous figure. A halo of sun, fog and mist created a surrealistic and supernatural sphere around the head and the raised arm. Her bust high above the clouds, her anxious eyes staring to the distance as though awaiting those coming this way so that she could guide them safely home. In an angelic and welcoming portrayal of what she represented. An audible gasp of delight and surprise unanimously escaped the lips of many enthralled by the sight.

Spellbound, I cursed myself for not having a camera. I was reflecting on the appropriateness of the clausal sculpture with a heavenly aura when just as suddenly the fog covered it again and hid it from sight. I was mesmerized by the entirety of the occasion when I recalled an incident from the previous day and broke out in a loud laughter, startling those close to me.

I was on my way to a clinical rotation as part of my medical education. My school was in Staten Island, NY and I had to take the ferry every morning to Manhattan. As I have mentioned earlier, I was employed by the City of

NY Health Department to work in some of the health clinics around town on a part time basis while in training. My schedule changed often and the bureaucracy of the city government delayed my paychecks reaching me on time. The day before this foggy morning, I went to the payroll office in order to find a solution to my predicament. I entered the city building on Worth Street and was directed to the second floor. In a very large typing-room with many noisily conducting their work, I was pointed to a massively built and oversized black lady at the end of the room. Even from that distance, I could see her towering over the entire room. I started walking toward her and halfway across the room, a very loud deep baritone type voice snapped at me. I froze to the un-lady like order: "Don you come bothering me boy. I too busy for your problems."

I gave her a three-finger salute, made a military type about-face and walked out of the room. I could hear loud giggles and laughter behind me. I walked down the stairs, out into the street and around the corner to a candy/card shop I had passed on my way in. I bought the biggest bright red box of chocolate and returned to the building. Outside the room I removed it from its bag and held it tray like high over my right shoulder and walked into the room. A loud chorus of laughter shook the room as I slowly and deliberately walked to the back of the room. My very large lady –now my friend– laughed heartily, snatched the box from my hand and shoved it into a desk drawer.

"Wauch you needs houney?"

Her entire side of the room seemed trashed with bundles of files everywhere. I wondered how she could possibly find anything. I had a long conversation with her as she expertly and knowledgeably looked up my file through volumes of ledgers and time cards – there were no computers in the early seventies. In the process I found out that she was an emigrant from Jamaica and had been here for some years with her family. After much runaround, she had finally got a Green Card and landed her job with the City as a bookkeeper.

She was well over six feet tall with a massive, yet attractive build. Once she learned that I was a medical student, she bombarded me with gamut of questions to most of which I had no answer.

She became a very helpful acquaintance who not only helped me but also my other classmates who worked for the City. She had three children. Her teenage daughter of nineteen was engaged to be married and actually in the following summer, I was one of a handful of white people invited to her lavish, Caribbean style wedding. To this day, it was one of the most memorable days in my life.

I felt dwarfed among her tall family and friends. Most of whom were from the islands, spoke with a thick accent and laughed at me for not understanding them. Lots of them had medical questions but I dodged them by telling them that I was just a student. The questions however were different from what I was hearing on daily bases from the patients I saw at the clinics. It was not till years later, that I heard those same health complains when I worked in the tropical regions of the world. Many of the guests at the wedding had traveled from Jamaica for the wedding, thus the unique questions.

So it was that the Goddess-like view of Lady Liberty that morning reminded me of my encounter with the lady at the government office and how people like her found their way to this land of ours. So many of the likes of her made countless and priceless contributions to our freedom. In the clinic, I worked at that day for example, we saw many patients from all walks of life and from all corners of the world. The majority of people working at that clinic too were immigrants. Several languages were spoken there and my colleagues' understanding of our patient population's cultures and particular medical issues made it possible for us to treat them effectively and appropriately.

Today, when I hear those who beat their chest with a protectionism fervor and claim ownership of this country, I remember that day and her and the gift of freedom bestowed on us all. How the rising torch of our Lady lights the way for all who need it. For the message on the Statue of Liberty does not say; "Give me your poor, your homeless, your huddled masses, so that they can replace my people and take away their jobs and their money." Rather it unconditionally says:

"*... Here at our sea-washed, sunset gates shall stand*
a mighty woman with a torch, whose flame
is the imprisoned lightning, and her name
Mother of Exiles. *From her beacon-hand*
glows world-wide welcome; her mild eyes command
the air-bridged harbor that twin cities frame,
"Keep, ancient lands, your storied pomp!" cries she
with silent lips. "Give me your tired, your poor,
Your huddled masses yearning to breathe free,
The wretched refuse of your teeming shore,
Send these, the homeless, tempest-tost to me,
I lift my lamp beside the golden door!"

AVE MARIA

"Ave Maria, gratia plena, Dominus tecum" goes the song in Latin. "Hail Mary, full of grace, the Lord is with thee" is the meaning of; perhaps the most widely sung religious song in the world. It is sung in many languages including Chinese, Arabic, and by many singers from Maria Callas to Frank Sinatra to Pavarotti & Bono to Celine Dion. It was originally written and composed in 1825 by Franz Schubert.

It is always sung with full passion and fervor, regardless of religious belief. I once heard a version of it sung in Hawaiian that seemed to reach deep into the soul and calm all insecurities in its path. Its collective message of prayer for peace is desired by all humanity. Today, with the many problems in the world, such a prayer seems most appropriate. If there is *one* individual in history who is loved and revered by all, it is the Lady Mary, daughter of Anne, mother of Jesus. Her selfless devotion and silent actions of goodness have done more for mankind than most sermons and speeches of others. Which brings us to the question, if the world can love and revere one such person, why can't we follow her example and care for each other better?

People don't hurt differently, babies don't cry in different languages, and the homeless don't despair differently in the Arctic or the Sahara. All the walls and borders of the world cannot isolate a mother's lament or a baby's hungry cry.

We can ease people's despair. Let's start by bringing peace to ourselves, our neighbors and fellow human beings. As healthcare providers, let's resolve to volunteer our services to the needy a few hours a week or a month. By using Telehealth, Telemedicine, and Tele-education, we don't even need to leave home.

Let's pray for peace for ALL during these trying times; *Ave Maria, Full of grace...*

Amen

In conclusion, it is important to know that the art of medicine has been around ever since mankind's existence and time itself. We should not allow today's technology or corporate greed to dictate how we practice it. Nor should we allow ourselves to lose our compassion and kindness in its digital quagmire and materialistic demands.

Computer technology allows us to spread our knowledge and understanding of this art. Along with it, our compassion too needs to carry across.